CALIFORNIA

WINE LOVERS' COOKBOOK

Other Books by The Wine Appreciation Guild

CALIFORNIA
WINE LOVERS' COOKBOOK

BY

MALCOLM HÉBERT

PUBLISHED BY

WINE APPRECIATION GUILD

WITH

WINE INSTITUTE

Wine Lovers' Cookbook
by Malcolm Hébert

Published by
The Wine Appreciation Guild
360 Swift Avenue
South San Francisco CA 94080
(800) 231-9463
www.wineappreciation.com

Library of Congress Catalog Number: 83-60779
ISBN: 0-932664-82-2
Book Design: Ronna Nelson
Cover Design: Jeffrey Caldewey
Cover Art: Joann Ortega
Editor: Brian St. Pierre
Asst. Editors: Marshal Newman, Donna Bottrell and Jean Valentine
Recipe Judges: Ed Borowiec, Malcolm Hébert, Millie Howie,
Jerry Mead, Rick Theis and others

Thirteenth Printing 2004

"We hear of the conversion of water into wine at the marriage, in Cana, as a miracle. But this conversion is, through the goodness of God, made every day before our eyes. Behold the rain, which descends from Heaven upon our vineyards, and which enters into the vine-roots to be changed into wine; a constant proof that God loves us and loves to see us happy."

—Benjamin Franklin

TABLE OF CONTENTS

FOREWORD

Food and wine are an inevitable combination. The cultural heritage of wine at the table reaches back through the centuries to the cradle of civilization. And today, with gracious dining and moderation an integral part of our lifestyle, more and more people are rediscovering the pleasures of wine with food.

There is no question but that California has had a great influence on the American consumer's rediscovery of both good food and good wine. The great agricultural heart of the state supplies the country with the essential ingredients for fine cooking, and California's wine industry produces harvest after harvest of extraordinary wine to enhance that food.

This cookbook is the result of a recipe contest sponsored by Wine Institute. The tremendous national response to the contest indicates more clearly than any survey the consumer's understanding and appreciation of wine and food, both in the kitchen and at the table. The recipes which appear represent the finest of those received, as judged by a group of food and wine writers here in California. We wish to thank all those who contributed, and we hope that this book will foster greater enjoyment of food and wine in the years to come.

John De Luca
President
Wine Institute

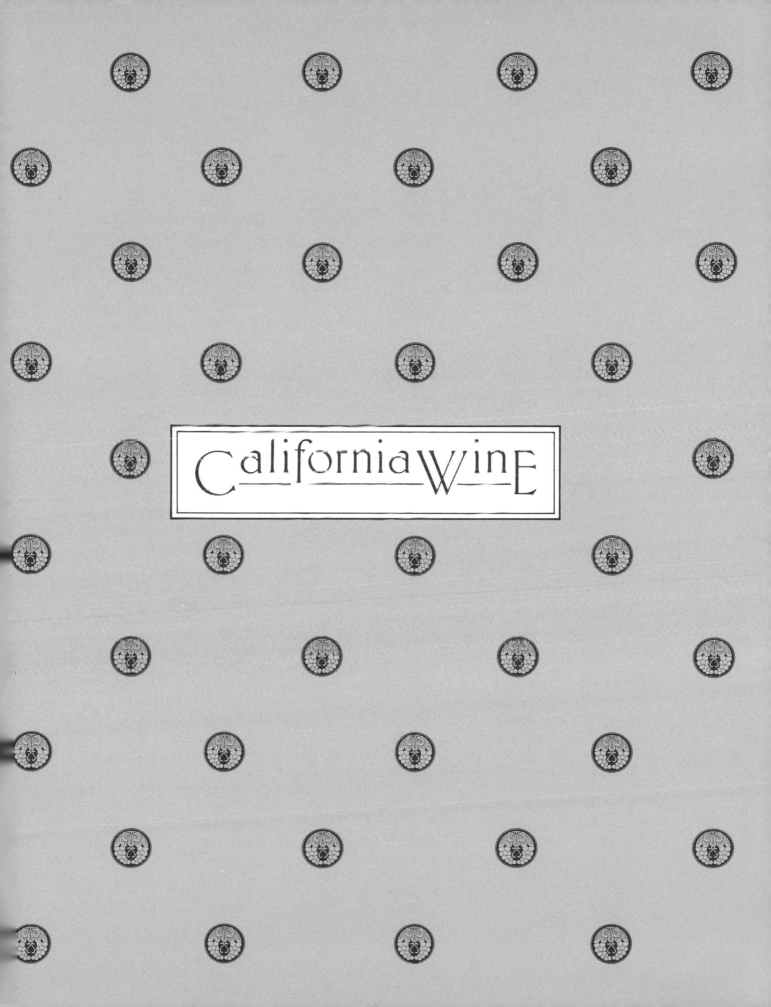

California Wine

CALIFORNIA WINE: THE STATE OF THE ART, THE ART OF THE STATE

Lately things have settled down a bit in California winemaking, permitting us to venture forth, like so many groundhogs in February, coming up for air and sunshine and vinous delights. The reason for this is that in the past few years, the supply of fine wine grapes has increased and something like a consensus on winemaking styles has begun to emerge.

California winemakers marched to different drummers in the past, often because there was no other music available; now we have something like an orderly parade, though still with room for determined soloists. The discord, frequent and considerable, lies in the past.

Then to Now

The California wine industry is over 200 years old, but it is just emerging from its infancy, having had more than its share of disruptions. Some of these were natural, like the devastation caused by the root louse phylloxera, others have been manmade, like the disastrous experiment of Prohibition. But in the relatively short time since Repeal, it has come a long way.

It began with a heroic effort by Father Junipero Serra and a band of settlers who established a chain of missions and settlements from San Diego to Sonoma. They grew grapes and made wine from the start. Other winemakers emigrated here from Europe, a tradition that continues to this day; you have only to look at the labels and see how much of a melting pot the California wine industry is.

The completion of the coast-to-coast railroad in 1876 gave California wine access to something like a national market, although (then and now) they had to overcome some prejudices back East.

But they made friends. One was Robert Louis Stevenson, who spent a happy year in the Napa Valley and wrote prophetically, "The smack of California earth shall linger on the palate of your grandson."

And there were others. By the time California wines were winning gold medals at European expositions at the turn of the century, it wasn't as great a shock as it might have been earlier.

The industry produced about 25-million gallons a year then, and the per capita consumption in America was about four-tenths of a gallon. In the first decade of this century, it increased to almost a gallon. It looked as if America were on the way to becoming a wine-drinking nation.

But the Prohibition movement was spreading. First towns and counties, then whole states, went dry. At first, wine was properly not included—it was a *temperance* movement. But as it widened, so did its targets, and wine was swept along with the tide.

In 1934, at Repeal, the California wine industry was worse off than it had ever been before, and there were no rainbows on the horizon.

Something had happened that reshaped the wine market. A generation of budding wine-drinkers had been nipped. The Jazz Age had run right into the Depression, neither one hospitable to the unhurried pleasures of table wines with meals. For the first time in the history of the industry, fortified sweet wines were produced in larger volume than traditional table wines, and that ratio persisted for another generation.

Leon Adams, in his book "The Wines of America," said it best: The wine industry was "making the wrong kinds of wines from the wrong kinds of grapes for the wrong kind of consumers in a whiskey-drinking nation with guilt feelings about imbibing in general and a confused attitude toward wine in particular."

But people—winemakers and consumers alike—began to learn. The University of California at Davis put together what has become one of the best schools of viticulture and enology in the world. Once and for all, California wine was on its way, though it was to be a long race.

A few figures will provide an idea of the scope of that achievement, as well as indicating, perhaps, how far we have to go.

In 1934, California wineries shipped 26-million gallons of wine to market. In 1941, it was 89-million, almost four times as much. In 1960, it was 129-million, and dessert wines had leveled off while table wines began a rise that hasn't peaked yet. In 1969, table wine outsold the sweet fortified wines for the first time, and what some people call the "wine boom" began. In the last ten years, shipments of California wine have nearly doubled, with table wines accounting for two-thirds of the total.

However, per capita consumption is only a little more than two gallons annually. If you compare that with an average of over 20 gallons annually in Italy and France, you can

see where we stand. We can put it in perspective this way: If you drank one glass of wine with your dinner every day, your per capita consumption would be 17 gallons a year.

Mise en Place

There is a wide range of soils in California, including gravelly, chalky and volcanic; those who subscribe to the notion that vines must struggle to produce the fruit for great wines would be gratified to see the labors of many California mountain vines.

Probably more important, California has a range of climatic conditions corresponding to the other great wine-producing regions of the world, from the Rhine to the Douro.

In 1971, in response to the quickening of the wine market, a great many new vines were planted. Much of this activity occurred in Monterey County, which had good soil and weather patterns, but unpredictable rainfall and water tables. With the advent of overhead-sprinkler and drip-irrigation systems, the problem was solved, and Monterey County joined the ranks, with one-sixth of California's new acreage.

Overall, over 180,000 acres of new vines were planted until 1975, when a combination of drought and a slightly sluggish wine market slowed the thrust. By the late 1970s, the impact of much of this new planting was felt, as yields of many varieties increased; some, such as Chardonnay, Gewurztraminer, Sauvignon Blanc and Johannisberg Riesling, actually doubled. As demand was again on the rise, this new supply came just in time.

Now we can ask, what is the state of the winemaking art in California?

Vino Verities

Conventional wisdom has it that varietal labeling, in which the wine is named for the principal grape, began in the 1940s; in fact, there were quite a few Zinfandels and Cabernet Sauvignons here over 100 years ago. Most wines were, however, what we call semi-generics, bearing such names as Burgundy and Chablis, though always preceded by "California." A hundred years ago, we also had "Medoc," "Hock," "Mosel," "St. Julien" and others. The trend has been toward simplification over the years and today we have a good deal of "white" or "red table wine," and the like.

With the increase of fine wine acreage, the quality of these blends has improved; the wines have become fruitier and a trifle drier.

Let Hugh Johnson, author of "The World Atlas of Wine," tell it: "If God had set about creating the ideal mealtime drink for America (which, I suppose, is pretty much what He did), California wine, the sort bottled in gallon and half-gallon jugs for national distribution, is the best answer you could expect even Him to come up with. At this level there is scarcely a comparison to make: Europe (alas!) has nothing to match California's jug wines for quality and value."

Varietal wines again became a trend in the 1940s, and thirty years later began showing up in half-gallon and gallon jugs, providing a clear boost to California winemaking and to consumers.

The varietal idea provides the clues to the styles and approaches of much of California winemaking. Therefore, the thing to do is to examine the most popular.

THE REDS

Barbera

Barbera may not be received as a leading actor, but quite often is more than a supporting player. Originally from the Piedmont region of Italy, in California it is tart, slightly astringent and rather assertive, with a mildly spicy aftertaste. California Barbera appears in two different styles—grapes grown in cooler areas tend to produce wines that are forward and robust, while grapes from the warmer San Joaquin Valley produce milder, somewhat less acidic and hard versions. The first can take a few years of aging, while the second are usually ready when you find them.

Obviously, they are an excellent match with Italian food, game, sausages and the like.

Cabernet Sauvignon

Little need be added to the firmly established reputation of Cabernet Sauvignon, a grape which has been made into some of the most celebrated and sought-after red table wines in the world, except to reiterate that many consider it the "king" of all red wine grapes. Grown around the world, it has distinguished itself in Bordeaux and California.

(Besides Cabernet Sauvignon, the Cabernet family includes three other noteworthy members—Cabernet Franc and Merlot, two important blending varieties, and Ruby Cabernet, developed in California by crossing Cabernet Sauvignon and Carignane, both members of the *Vitis Vinfera* family of wine grapes.)

Without doubt, Cabernet Sauvignons and Chardonnays have provided notable proof of California's success; a number of comparative tastings in America and abroad have affirmed the doctrine of different-but-equal.

Flavor associations that come up with the wine demonstrate the austere quality of it: Herbaceous, green-olive, fresh green peppers, tea-like and, in California at least, a note of mint-eucalyptus. No indication of easy charms here . . . And yet, ten years after the vintage, even twenty in some cases, it becomes a wine you can meet with straightforward affability, a perfect match for a roast leg of lamb or prime rib.

Many California Cabernets are 100 percent of the variety; in France its cousins Merlot and Cabernet Franc are blended in to soften the wine, make it a trifle more accessible. With very little Merlot available (just over 100 acres in 1967), California winemakers were forced to adopt a style which became a considerable virtue in its own right, an informal elegance that is uniquely Californian, and no less accessible.

Now there are over 4,000 acres of Merlot standing, and we have seen more experiments with various blends in the past few years.

Gamay and Gamay Beaujolais

The two grapes are not relatives, though in France they were neighbors, at least. The Gamay Beaujolais turns out to be a misidentified strain of Pinot Noir; Gamay, sometimes also called Napa Gamay, turns out to be the "true" grape of Beaujolais.

The matter is not as complicated as it could be, simply because both grapes are vinified into light and lively wines meant for easy and early drinking, with more similarities than differences between them.

These fruity and unassuming wines make a good match with unassuming foods, including picnics. Half an hour in the refrigerator will bring them to a cool temperature that emphasizes their piquancy and affinity with light lunches and dinners on a warm day.

There has also been a trend lately to bring out some Gamay Beaujolais in the Nouveau style, between six and eight weeks after the harvest. They are delightfully smooth.

Petite Sirah

Confusions of nomenclature continue with this grape, though not so much with the wines it has produced in recent years. For those who look for the evidence in the glass, it

will not matter much; for the others, here is a brief digression:

Much, but by no means all, of what had been identified as Petite Sirah, turned out to be a similar grape called the Duriff, originally from the Rhone. So is the Sirah, which already had as tangled a parentage as any Dickens hero in its home country. Like both those grapes, Petite Sirah was long considered a blending grape, and provided backbone for many a California Burgundy.

About fifteen years ago, it began to come into its own as a varietal, and there can be little doubt that there were a number of witting and unwitting Duriff/Sirah blends. Inevitably, however, California winemakers have gone their way and evolved a distinct style that makes botany and comparisons somewhat moot. Some blending may be done (but not nearly so much as in the Rhone), but the character of the variety shines through strongly.

California Petite Sirahs are generally medium-to-full-bodied, deep in color, astringent, and possess a slight spiciness in the finish—a refreshing aftertaste. Time in the bottle is a good idea; no one can be sure of the eventual longevity of many of them, as the field is so new, but there is a great deal of promise here.

Food to match its fullness is called for; this is a wine for game and lamb if ever there was one.

Pinot Noir

For a long while, if anyone had asked what kind of food went with Pinot Noir, the answer might have been, "Red herring." In the unfolding California wine drama, Pinot Noir was seen as a villain by some and a hero by a few others, but, with a few exceptions, usually turned out to be neither.

Around the world, Pinot Noir is a difficult grape, unforgiving of the least casualness in any step along the way to fine wine. It is genetically unstable, reproducing odd variations within itself; it is prone to most ailments a vine can suffer; growing conditions must just fit its requirements; and then, when its moment of truth arrives, its balky and temperamental fermentation is enough to give winemakers fits.

So why bother? Simply because of the fact that when it's good, it's very, very good.

The first steps toward achieving that goodness with consistency began in the Sixties, with the sorting of all the odd clones that had developed; the better variations were then planted in cooler areas, where growing conditions suited it well, especially in recent

vintages. As the vines mature, we should have a good idea what the wines will become—the early evidence is excellent.

California Pinot Noirs tend to be ample and fleshy, soft, even velvety in the mouth. Recent versions have tended to a shade more tannin in an attempt to introduce more complexity and aging potential.

Zinfandel

The origins of Zinfandel—often billed as "California's mystery grape"—are obscure, but there is no mystery to its popularity: Quite simply, it can make awfully good wine, in a variety of styles. It's safe to say that there is a Zinfandel for everyone's taste.

Currently, hundreds of wineries in California produce Zinfandel; from Mendocino to San Diego (and every other place in between where grapes grow), it flourishes.

Zinfandel actually put California on the wine map over 100 years ago. Much of the state's wine-grape acreage for many years had been devoted to the Mission grape, which was originally brought in by Father Junipero Serra in 1769. The Mission yielded a merely passable table wine, and Zinfandel quickly replaced it by the 1880s. It accounted for 40 percent of all grapevines in California.

The grape was apparently introduced in the 1850s in California, possibly as a table grape. As soon as it was turned into wine, however, people knew they were onto a good thing. A Zinfandel won first prize in the California state fair in 1859, another made by Count Agoston Harazsthy won first prize in a fair in 1864, and several others followed.

After Repeal, it was more of a workhorse wine than a thoroughbred, but being the second most widely planted winegrape in California, it had the attention of discerning winemakers, and eventually consumers.

Until 1966, most Zinfandels were made in a light style which led to its early reputation as "America's Beaujolais." The characterization is more handy than accurate— Zinfandel is rather more tart than Beaujolais—but it helped people accept the foundling.

An important change was the flood of newcomers to the California wine scene around that time. Some of them had idiosyncratic ideas, like making Zinfandels with blockbuster strength that might age for ten or twenty years and aim to rival Cabernets for the "claret" championship of America.

In assessing the state of the Zinfandel art today, it seems best to characterize it in two broad strokes. The first are the light and fruity wines meant to be consumed fairly young, and which evoke the "Beaujolais" image. They share a lightness in body and a garnet color. The flavor is usually characterized as "bramble" (really another name for wild blackberries), the aroma is distinctly fruity; uncomplicated by much tannin, the flavor keeps coming back at you with every sip, like a friendly puppy.

The next class comes on a little stronger; dark ruby wines with hints of oak aging, and a slight astringency testifying fermentation in contact with the skins long enough to build a structure under the familiar berryish fruitiness. These wines edge into claret territory. Most of them are moderately priced and the spine of many a California wine cellar.

A winemaker once told me that Zinfandel ferments so easily that it almost seems eager to turn into wine; tasting it, in any of its variations, you can see why. After over 100 years in the cocoon, it's turned into quite a butterfly.

THE WHITES

Chardonnay

As the idea of California Chardonnay being able to challenge great white Burgundies is only a bit more than twenty years old, it must be regarded as something of a prodigy as we consider the evidence at hand.

Chardonnay was not planted extensively around the state for a long time—there were a mere 1,412 acres in 1967. One reason was that they were prone to a number of viruses; with the help of UC Davis, this problem was eased and the way was clear.

The other development was the use of French oak barrels; there had been some use of oak before for California wines, including American oak and even old whiskey barrels way back when. But new oak cooperage, not just from France, but Burgundy itself, was a revelation and the beginning of a revolution. Chardonnay got glamor—and sold.

It also began some controversy which has not settled yet. Essentially, there are three styles of Chardonnay in California today. The first is a group of powerhouse wines, heavily oaked, relatively high in alcohol (thirteen percent), with rich, ripe fruitiness; the second subdues the oak and alcohol in favor of a supple, tart fruitiness (in this day and age, can one say that the former is "masculine" while the latter is "feminine"?); the third style is the "if you want to taste wood, go bite a tree" approach: no oak.

Surprisingly, though oak is supposed to build an underlying structure in the wine that aids graceful aging, many of these no-oak wines have held up beautifully for five or six years.

Taken together, these styles offer a good look at the possibilities of the wine. Incidentally, the grape and wine are also sometimes called Pinot Chardonnay, but the grape is not a member of the Pinot family.

Chenin Blanc

Chenin Blanc occupies much the same position in the white-wine spectrum as Zinfandel does in the red; it is abundant, and made in slightly differing styles by a lot of wineries.

In all its incarnations, it is a light and fruity wine meant to be enjoyed for its youthful charms; its aroma is almost flowery. The comparison, if one must be made, is with the wines of the Loire, especially Vouvray.

The most popular style is to make the wine as fresh and fruity as possible, with just a touch of residual sugar—a wine for lazy sipping and light lunches. An up-and-coming style is to ferment the wine dry, but no less fruity, which makes it a good companion for chicken and even simply prepared fish.

Gewurztraminer

The keynote of this wine is an incredible spiciness, as if of a hillside where herbs and wildflowers grow together in profusion. In California, partly because of a bit more sun, partly by design, the wine is softer and more flowery than its Alsatian counterpart.

However, much of the newer plantings are in new areas for the vine, and some of the grapes end up in the hands of newer winemakers, so generalizations are somewhat difficult. The consensus appears at the moment to be leaning toward a balance of sugar and spice in a moderately light wine, suitable as an aperitif with mild cheeses, or with chicken in any light or sweet sauce.

Johannisberg Riesling

Around 100 years ago, wine called Riesling was made in California; when the grape of the Rhine and Mosel was planted here it was dubbed "Johannisberg" Reisling to mark its identity. The proper name of the variety is White Riesling, but a lot of it went unsold when people tried to so label it.

For quite some time, perhaps waiting for other grapes to fill the void, Johannisberg Riesling in California was drier, fuller-bodied and much more assertive all around than its German cousins, a wine that could march up to even seafood as a peer. A number are still made that way and quite intriguing in their own right.

A while ago, a lighter and slightly sweet style began to emerge, and a number of newer winemakers with new acreage have joined this school with fragrant and fruity wines.

Additionally, *Botrytis cinerea,* the so-called Noble Mold, has begun to appear with some frequency in California (or perhaps it was always here but not recognized); the resulting wines are rich and sweet, known as "Late Harvest" wines on California labels, and are wonderful accompaniments to dessert.

Sauvignon Blanc

Would Judy Garland have been a star under her real name, Frances Gumm? We may never know, but we do know that's what happened to Sauvignon Blanc when it grabbed the spotlight as Fumé Blanc about 10 years ago.

This came as no surprise to the experts at U.C. Davis, who had been extolling its virtues for years. It shares some of the grassy, herbaceous flavor quality of its Cabernet Sauvignon cousin; the "fumé" idea is said to come more from the smoky appearance of the grapes at harvest-time than as a flavor association, but there are those who think of it as such. Its immense popularity added luster to the family name in the happy end.

There is a fair consensus here on what the wine ought to be—dry, fresh and bracing; it is extraordinarily versatile in combination with food, from poultry to seafood to lighter meats.

Miscellaneous

Emerald Riesling, Grey Riesling, Sylvaner and Pinot Blanc all make light and lovely wines which are neither gaining nor declining in popularity or acreage planted. French Colombard, with the advent of cold fermentation, is definitely a winner and in good supply.

The Coda of the West

There is much more—a minor revolution in Rosés, new *cuvées* for sparkling wines, white wines from red grapes, absolutely marvelous California Ports and Sherries—the list is not endless, it only seems that way. California wine is high adventure for those with open minds and palates.

Brian St. Pierre
Wine Institute

ENTERTAINING WITH WINE AND CHEESE

The marriage of wine and cheese is a long and happy one, and a good way to celebrate it is an easy and inexpensive wine-and-cheese tasting party.

The question immediately arises: What sort of cheeses are compatible with various wines? The following list provides some basic guidelines, though of course your palate should be the final arbiter.

Here are some other helpful hints:

Serve a variety of cheese types. It's certainly possible to give a cheddar-tasting party, for example, but most people prefer to taste cheeses which are unlike each other.

Mix bland and strong-flavored cheeses, familiar and rarer cheeses. Serving all mild cheeses could be boring, and too many full-flavored cheeses might tire the palate.

Serve cheeses at room temperature. Creamy cheeses need be taken from the refrigerator only half an hour ahead; for most others, an hour is about right. White and Rosé wines should of course be chilled.

The cheeses reflect a broad range of international tastes; the wines chosen are from California, not only for their preeminent quality and value, but also because they represent the same range of diversity.

Accompanying crackers or breads should not be salty or too spicy, and there shouldn't be too much of a variety, so as not to mix up the palate, confounding the other flavors.

CHEESE	WINE
Cheddars New York, Vermont or Wisconsin Cheddar, Cheshire, Caerphilly, Double Gloucester, Colby, Longhorn, Monterey Jack	Ruby Cabernet, California Burgundy, Gamay Beaujolais, California Dry Sherry
Moderately Firm, Mild Gouda, Munster, Tilsit, Danbo, Tybo, Edam, Esrom, Port du Salut, Bel Paese, Havarti, Bon Bel, Fontina	Zinfandel, California Gamay, Pinot Chardonnay, Johannisberg Riesling
Emmenthal American, Austrian or Swiss Swiss, Samsoe, Gruyere, Jarlsberg	French Colombard, California Chablis, Chenin Blanc, Rosé
Blues Roquefort, Danish or American Blue, Gorgonzola, Stilton	California Port, Pinot Noir, Barbera
White or Creamy Cheeses Boursin, Feta, Boursault, Grape Cheese, Taleggio, Gourmandise	Grey Riesling, Sauvignon or Fumé Blanc, Gewurztraminer
Brie, Camembert, Pont L'Eveque	Petite Sirah, Cabernet Sauvignon

Cooking With Wine

COOKING WITH WINE

Wine has been man's cooking companion for more years than gastronomic historians can record. The first grapes cultivated by man were probably grown in Asia Minor, south of the Black and Caspian Seas, between 6,000 and 4,400 B.C. (The Bible gives credit to Noah as the first viticulturist, just nine generations after Adam.) Cultivation of the vines spread all around the Mediterranean. The Phoenicians introduced vines into Greece, Rome and eventually France. Vines were also cultivated by the people of Mesopotamia, the ancient Egyptians, the Babylonians and the Sumerians.

The ancients found that wine was not only an enjoyable beverage, but had special medicinal properties, and could be used as a restorative and sedative. It was added to water as a purifying agent in regions where the water supply might be unsafe. Foodstuffs were washed in wine and kept edible in a marinade of wine, oil and herbs. Wounds were cleaned with wine.

The vines spread and spread; the Carthaginians, Etruscans and later the Romans established vineyards and made wine throughout Italy. However, local vineyards, whether a private vineyard or a large-scale plantation, could not keep up with the demand of the far-flung Roman Empire, so the armies of Rome planted vineyards where they conquered—in and around Bordeaux and the Rhone river in France and the Mosel valley in Germany, for example.

California had a gentler conqueror; in July of 1769, a Franciscan missionary, Father Junipero Serra, planted the first vines. While those vines around the Mission San Diego de Alcala were growing, he also brought sacramental wine from Mexico.

That first crush must have been a festive affair. The juice was crushed from the grapes by Indians treading on cowhides stretched across poles and piled high with the ripe fruit. Tanks caught the fresh juice for fermentation. If you visit this Mission today, you can find the remains of that primitive wine-making. By now, the world knows how far we've come from that beginning.

In ancient times, cooks used wine by trial and error; they had no one to tell them how much wine should be used in various dishes. Fortunately, we have a monitoring system that helps today's chef to use the right amount of California wines in a host of dishes.

But before you use this handy guide, here are some hints about employing wine in the kitchen that you should be aware of when planning your menus.

● After a bottle of wine has been opened, the unused portion can be safely stored in the refrigerator for about one week.

● If you buy wines by the gallon, decant them into fifths and reseal or recork them. They will keep longer.

● If your family members are not hearty wine drinkers and there is a little left over in the bottle, use it the next day in a salad as a replacement for vinegar.

● A chef's trick is to mix yesterday's leftover wine with an equal amount of melted butter which becomes today's basting sauce for roasts, game or poultry. Add to the basting sauce your own favorite herbs and spices.

MATCHING FOODS AND WINES

If you want to start an argument among people, do as I do and state boldly and with total conviction that you like charcoal-broiled steak with ice cold California Champagne.

What you are going to get are the old clichés, such as "I thought red wines were meant for red meats!" Well, yes. Some meats might well demand a big, robust red wine. On the other hand a classic French dish, Truite en Chambertin, is trout cooked in red wine. Would you drink a white wine with this dish?

The best advice anyone can give you about matching foods and wines is as follows:

● Try the rules and see if they please your palate. The rules state that red wine goes with red meat, white wine with white meat, rosé is for luncheons and Champagne is the all-purpose wine.

● If you don't like the above rules, start making a few of your own. In this way you will please your palate and not worry about what the other people like, think or say about your tastes.

Remember one thing. You have some 10,000 taste buds inside your mouth. What you like is a product of what your mother and father served you as you grew up. Your parents were influenced by what your grandparents served your parents. Other influences on your palate are what you ate at relatives' and friends' homes.

Yet no one lives inside your mouth but you, and that means that you alone are the final judge of what foods you like with what wines. Of course, you should experiment. And if you find your tastes are changing, then make that change. After all, it is you who must be satisfied.

WINE COOKING GUIDE

FOODS	AMOUNT OF WINE	TYPE OF WINE
SOUPS		
Clear	1 tablespoon per cup	Dry sherry
Cream	1 tablespoon per cup	Dry sherry
Meat	1 tablespoon per cup	Red wine, champagne
Vegetable	1 tablespoon per cup	White wine, red wine
SAUCES		
Cream (no eggs)	1 tablespoon per cup	Brandy, dry sherry
Cream (with eggs)	1½ tablespoons per cup	Brandy, dry sherry
Brown (thin)	1 tablespoon per cup	Red Wine
Brown (thick)	1½ tablespoons per cup	Red Wine
Tomato (not spicy)	1 tablespoon per cup	Red wine
Tomato (spicy)	2 tablespoons per cup	Red wine
Cheese (mild)	1 tablespoon per cup	White wine
Cheese (strong)		None
MEATS		
Beef, lamb or veal	¼ cup per pound	Red or white wine, California brandy
Ham (baked/roasted)	1½ cups (basting)	Port, cream sherry
Pot roast	½ cup per pound	Red wine
Liver (sauteed)	¼ cup per pound	Red or white wine, California brandy
Innards (brains, kidneys, etc.)	2 tablespoons per half pound	White wine

FISH

Poached	½ cup per pound	White wine (dry)
Baked	½ cup per pound	White wine (dry)
Broiled		None, except in the sauce. See fish sauces in your favorite cookbook.
Grilled (charcoal)		Same as broiled
Sauteed	3 tablespoons per pound	White wine with 3 tablespoons lemon juice

POULTRY

Chicken (baked, poached, sauteed)	½ cup per pound	Red or white wine
Chicken (broiled, grilled)	Amount called for in the sauce	
Turkey	½ cup per pound	Same as for chicken

GAME

Pheasant	¼ to ½ cup per pound depending upon cooking method	Red wine, California brandy, sherry
Quail	¼ cup per pound	White wine, sherry
Cornish Game Hen	¼ cup per pound	Red wine, California brandy, port
Pigeon	½ cup per pound	Red wine, port
Partridge/Grouse	¼ cup per pound	White wine, port, California brandy
Venison	¼ cup per pound	Red wine

SHELLFISH

Mussels	¼ cup per pound	White wine
Shrimps	¼ cup per pound	White wine
Clams	¼ cup per pound	White wine
Lobsters	¼ cup per pound	White wine
Crawfish	¼ cup per pound	White wine

VEGETABLES

All	1/4 to 1/3 cup per pound	Red or white wine, brandy, port, cream sherry depending upon the recipe.

Appetizers

APPETIZERS

They have been called blotters, soakers, splashers, thumbbits, starters and canapes. The French call them hors d'oeuvres and the Americans call them appetizers.

No matter what you call them, those little morsels are finding their way back onto menus today. A few years ago, appetizers began to fade from the table. Now, with the accent on lighter meals, people are watching their waistlines and this is where appetizers play a major role. How? They help curb your appetite, so you do not eat as much.

Before you are introduced to the real world of appetizers, here are some hints that will help you plan your menu.

● If you are planning to serve a heavy dinner, the appetizers should be light; not more than three types.

● If you are planning a light dinner, serve three or more appetizers.

● The best wine to serve with appetizers is a brut or natural California Champagne, or if you prefer a California rosé Champagne. All are elegant for parties.

SWEDISH MEAT BALLS

1 cup soft bread crumbs
7/8 cup milk
1 lb. ground round
1 egg, well beaten
1 Tbs. minced onion
1/4 tsp. mace
1/8 tsp. allspice
1 tsp. sugar
1/8 tsp. pepper
3 Tbs. bacon drippings
4 Tbs. flour
1-10 oz. can condensed consomme
1 cup California white wine
1/2 cup undiluted evaporated milk
2 Tbs. chopped parsley

Soak bread crumbs (fresh bread) in milk for 5 to 10 minutes. Put in bowl. Add beef, beaten egg, onion, mace, allspice and salt and pepper. Mix thoroughly. Heat bacon drippings in a large, heavy skillet. With wet hands, shape mixture into balls about the size of a walnut. Brown balls nicely on all sides. (They will flatten somewhat.) Try to work fast so that the drippings will not burn—take out the ones that are done and add more to brown as there is room. Remove balls from pan. Add flour to the drippings in the skillet and blend well. Add the consomme gradually until it is all blended, with a low heat. Add wine in the same manner. Add evaporated milk. Cook, stirring constantly until mixture is thickened and smooth. Add parsley, and taste for seasoning. Return balls to gravy, cover skillet and simmer gently for about 20 minutes. May be transferred to a chafing dish to keep warm. Makes about 36 meat balls. Serve with rice or noodles. Serves 6.

Lilli Malork of Vallejo, California uses a dry California white wine with mace and allspice to liven up these meatballs.

HOT CHEDDAR SPREAD

*1 lb. extra-sharp Cheddar cheese,
  grated
8 oz. cream cheese, softened
1/2 cup prepared horseradish
1 tsp. Tobasco sauce
2 tsps. Worcestershire sauce
1 Tbs. cream
1/2 cup California medium dry
  Sherry*

Blend cheddar and cream cheeses together until well mixed. (This can be done in a bowl with a wooden spoon, but using a food processor will produce a smoother product and a less severe case of cook's elbow.) Add remaining ingredients and blend until smooth. Taste mixture and adjust seasonings to personal preference. If a "hotter" spread is desired, increase horseradish, not Tobasco. Place cheese spread in containers and refrigerate. Spread will last for months if kept tightly covered and refrigerated. Serves 12.

Cheese has long been established as a "must" for a first course. Bob Duncan of Rhineback, New York obviously likes it hot.

ENGLISH POTTED CHEESE

*1 lb. Cheshire or Double
   Gloucester, grated
6 Tbs. softened butter
1/2 tsp. mace
dash of pepper
dash of dry mustard
1/2 cup California cream Sherry*

Combine ingredients in the order given, and beat until smooth. Place in a crock or pot, cover with waxed paper pressed over the cheese under the lid. Keep in refrigerator for at least 24 hours. Makes 2 cups. Serve with a variety of crackers. Serves 12.

There are many recipes for the famed English appetizer potted cheese. Barbara Ericson of Loomis, California makes this version simple but tasty.

PEARL'S PALATE PLEASERS

1 lb. cream cheese (or Neufchatel)
1/4 lb. (one stick) sweet butter
1/8 pound Roquefort cheese
1 can skinless and boneless
  sardines, drained
3 inches anchovy paste from tube
1 clove garlic, minced
1/4 medium large sweet onion,
  minced
1 Tbs. dijon mustard
1 cup California Chenin Blanc

Allow cheeses and butter to come to room temperature. Mash all ingredients together, using food processor or blender. Place mixture in covered container in refrigerator allowing 24 hours for flavors to meld. Use as a dip with a platter of cut vegetables (crudities) or as a spread with melba toast or bland crackers. Serve with white or red California wine, according to preference. As the mixture is rich, a dry wine is indicated. Serves 10.

Chicago wine lovers have enjoyed Pearl Powell's special dip, which can be served with crudities, crackers or toast. Now you can, too.

ITALIAN SAUSAGE MARINO

*2 lbs. sweet Italian sausage (or
one lb. sweet, and one lb. hot
sausage)*
2 Tbs. olive oil
1-8 oz. can tomato sauce
1 cup California dry red wine
*1 Tbs. minced fresh parsley or
1½ tsp. dried*
1/2 tsp. dried sweet basil
*1 Tbs. grated Romano or Locatelli
cheese*

Cut each link of sausage into four pieces. Add oil to skillet. Add sausage and start cooking on low heat until fat in sausage begins to melt. Then raise heat and brown sausage on all sides. Drain very thoroughly. Reserve sausage. Add tomato sauce, 1/2 cup wine, parsley, basil and grated cheese. Stir to loosen particles in skillet. Cover and simmer slowly for one hour, checking occasionally to be sure liquid has not boiled away. If necessary, add a little more wine. At end of cooking time, add remaining wine, bring quickly to a boil, then remove from heat. To serve hot: Place sausage in chafing dish and pour wine sauce over it. Serves 6. To serve cold: Refrigerate sausage in wine sauce overnight. Place a toothpick in each piece and arrange on platter with other snacks such as marinated artichoke hearts, black and green olives, cubes of provalone cheese, cherry tomatoes, and green pepper strips.

Italian sausage, served as a first course, is close to universal. In Tucson, Arizona Myra Marino cooks this recipe to tickle her friend's taste buds.

ARTICHOKE APPETIZER

1-8½ oz. can artichoke hearts or
bottoms, drained and finely
chopped
1 cup mayonnaise
1/2 cup California Chenin Blanc
1 cup grated Parmesan cheese
1/2 cup plain bread crumbs
1/4 tsp. white pepper
1/4 tsp. oregano

Preheat oven to 350 degrees. Drain artichokes, chop finely. Gradually add Chenin Blanc to mayonnaise, blending well. Fold in Parmesan cheese, bread crumbs, white pepper, oregano and chopped artichokes. Place in ungreased 1 quart baking dish and bake, uncovered for 25 to 30 minutes, until hot and bubbly. Serve hot with party bread, crackers or vegetables. Delicious spooned into fresh mushroom caps. Serves 8.

In America, artichokes are grown only in California; Barbara Jacome of Rocky Hill, Connecticut, offers this first course using the next best thing to fresh.

DELECTABLE DRUMSTICKS

15 chicken wings
1/2 cup honey
3 Tbs. cornstarch
1 tsp. seasoned salt
1/2 tsp. ground ginger
1/2 tsp. lemon pepper
1 chicken bouillon cube dissolved in
  3/4 cup hot water
1/3 cup California white wine
1/4 cup California cream Sherry

Cut tips off wings and cut wings in half by cutting through joint with a sharp knife or cleaver. Arrange wings on a broiler pan rack in a single layer. Bake in a hot oven 400 degrees for 25 to 30 minutes, turning once. Mix honey, cornstarch, salt, ginger, lemon pepper, chicken bouillon, and California white wine in a small saucepan. Simmer constantly until mixture thickens and boils 3 minutes. Remove from fire and brush over wings. When they are glazed and shiny remove to a chafing dish. Combine sauce and the cream Sherry and pour over chicken wings. Keep heating flame low. Makes 30 tiny drumsticks. Serves 6.

Chicken wings have become the best known appetizer to serve to your guests who arrive en masse. Mrs. Robert Ross of Sonora, California, offers this version.

WINE AND CHEESE BREAD

3 cups all-purpose flour
1 package dry yeast
1/2 cup California dry Sherry
3 eggs
1/2 cup butter or margarine
2 tsp. salt
2 tsp. sugar
1-1 1/2 cups (4-6 oz.) finely cubed
    Monterey jack cheese

In a large mixing bowl, combine 1 1/2 cups of the flour and the yeast. In a saucepan, heat wine, butter or margarine, sugar and salt until warm (115-120 degrees F), stirring constantly until butter is almost melted. Add to dry mixture in mixing bowl. Add eggs. Beat at low speed with electric mixer for 1/2 minute, scraping sides of bowl constantly, then at high speed for three additional minutes. By hand, stir in enough remaining flour to make a soft dough. Knead until smooth and elastic. Place in greased bowl, cover and let rise until double, about 1 1/2 hours. Punch dough down, work in cheese, cover and let rest 10 minutes. Shape into a round 8 inch loaf in a greased pie pan. Let rise until double, about 45 minutes. Bake at 375 degrees for 40 minutes, covering the top loosely with foil after the first 20 minutes.

Bread is not technically an appetizer. However, there is no reason not to enjoy this tasty bread before as well as during a meal. The recipe comes from Mrs. Lynn Seyfert of Idaho Falls, Idaho.

EGGPLANT OLE

*1 large (about 1 1/2 lbs.) eggplant,
  unpared
3 Tbs. salad oil
1 8 oz. can tomato sauce
2 cloves garlic, minced
1 medium green pepper, diced
1 medium onion, chopped
1 Tbs. ground cumin (yes, that's
  right!)
1/4 tsp. cayenne pepper
1 Tbs. honey
2 tsp. salt
1/4 cup California red wine
1 4¼ oz. can chopped ripe olives
1/4 cup chopped cilantro leaves
2 to 3 Tbs. California red table
  wine, or as needed*

Dice eggplant into small cubes. Heat oil in large skillet. Add eggplant and rest of ingredients except olives, cilantro and the 2 to 3 tablespoons wine. Cook, covered, over medium-low heat from 20 minutes, stirring occasionally. Uncover and continue cooking until thickened and reduce to about 3 cups. Add olives; cover and chill at least 2 hours. Before serving, add cilantro and red wine as needed for dipping consistancy. Serve with corn chips, tortilla strips, pita bread cut in triangles, or vegetable scoopers of celery, zucchini, green pepper or carrots. Makes about 3 cups.

A certificate of appreciation went to Nessie Valerie of Pico Rivera, California for her eggplant ole.

MEATBALLS IN RED WINE SAUCE

1 onion, finely chopped
1 cup bread crumbs
2 lbs. ground beef
3 eggs
1/2 tsp. salt
1/4 tsp. pepper
1/2 tsp. seasoned salt (optional)
3/4 cup Parmesan cheese
1/2 tsp. Worcestershire sauce
2 cloves garlic, diced
1 cup flour
2 Tbs. salad oil
1 cup California red wine
1/2 cup beef consomme
2-8 oz. cans tomato sauce
1/8 tsp. oregano

Mix the first ten ingredients plus one of the cloves of minced garlic together. Form into small meatballs. Roll lightly in flour. Place the salad oil and remaining garlic in a large skillet. Add meatballs and brown on all sides (several batches will be required). Meanwhile, combine remaining ingredients in a large saucepan and bring to simmering point. Add the meatballs and simmer together for about 25 to 35 minutes. Place in a chafing dish and serve with large toothpicks. Makes about 80 meatballs.

One of the perennial favorites at all parties are those delightful little meatballs that are served in a savory sauce. Irene Gross of Amston, Connecticut, serves them this creative way.

Soups

SOUPS

Soups are the chef's calling card. In fact, many great restaurants are judged on the way the chef de cuisine prepares the various soups he serves his guests. If the soup is great, tasty and worthy of a second helping, you can be somewhat assured that the remainder of the dinner will be just as great.

Wine has been an ingredient in soups for thousands of years. Gastronomic historians are not sure just when man ladled a spoonful of wine into his soup just to make it taste different, but ladle it he did.

There are no hard and fast rules about mixing wines in soups, only a few practical suggestions.

● Always use an everyday wine; soup is no place for a great one.

● Never use the so-called "cooking wines", because they can ruin a perfectly good dish with their saltiness.

● Experiment with various California wines, to find those which please your palate.

● Use the amount suggested in the recipe, and if it is too much for your palate, decrease the amount.

ICED MELON SOUP

3 cups cantaloupe, coarsely chopped
3 cups honeydew, coarsely chopped
2 cups orange juice, freshly
  squeezed
1/3 cup lime juice, freshly squeezed
3 Tbs. honey—or to taste according
  to sweetness of the melons
2 cups California Brut Champagne
  or dry California white wine
1 cup whipping cream (optional)
Fresh mint leaves

Finely chop 1 1/2 cup each of the cantaloupe and honeydew melon and set aside. Place remaining chopped cantaloupe and honeydew in blender with orange juice, lime juice and honey and puree. It will take only a few seconds. Pour into a large bowl. Stir in the champagne or wine and the reserved finely chopped melon. Chill in the refrigerator for several hours for the flavors to blend. To serve, pour into iced bowls or into large crystal wine glasses. Garnish with a drollop of whipped cream (if desired) and with fresh mint leaves. Serves 6 to 8.

A certificate of appreciation was captured by Barbara Karoff of Menlo Park, California for this summer soup.

VEGETARIAN LENTIL SOUP BURGUNDY

1/4 cup olive oil
1 large onion, chopped
2 ribs celery, chopped
1 clove garlic, chopped
1 cup lentils, rinsed
6 cups water
1 large carrot, shredded
1 large potato diced
1-16 oz. can tomatoes, chopped
1 cup California red wine
Salt and pepper
6 to 8 pimento stuffed olives, sliced
6 to 8 sprigs of parsley
1/4 cup chopped walnuts

In a large kettle, saute onion, celery and garlic in olive oil until lightly browned. Add lentils, water, carrot, potato, tomatoes, and wine. Cover and simmer one hour, or until lentils are tender. Just before serving, add salt and pepper to taste. Garnish each bowl with olive slices, chopped parsley, and about 1 teaspoonful of chopped walnuts. Serves 6-8.

Vegetarians, take note. A certificate of appreciation was awarded by the judges for an excellent soup. You can thank Alexandra Kazaks of Sarasota, Florida.

SHERRIED SPLIT PEA SOUP

2 cups dried split peas
2 quarts water
1 large onion, quartered
1 whole clove garlic
2 whole carrots
1 large stalk celery, with leaves
4 sprigs parsley
1 ham shank with meat
10 whole black peppercorns
1 bay leaf
2 cups light cream
1 to 2 cups milk
1/2 cup California dry Sherry
Salt and pepper to taste

Place first 10 ingredients in a heavy kettle. Cook over low heat, stirring occasionally, for 3 hours until peas are soft. Remove from heat. Remove ham from the bone, dice and set aside. (The dicing may be done in the food processor, using a steel knife.) Remove peppercorns, bay leaf, and if desired garlic. If garlic is not removed sieve or puree it with the other vegetables. Sieve onion, carrots, celery and parsley or puree them in the food processor with a steel knife. Return soup, ham, and puree to kettle. Add cream, milk and Sherry to desired thickness. Salt and pepper to taste. Simmer for 15 to 30 minutes to warm stirring often. Serves 8.

I like the way Betsy Fowler of Los Altos uses California Sherry in her pea soup.

FRUIT SOUP

2 cups sliced nectarines
1/2 cup sour cream
1/2 cup California Rosé wine

Put all the ingredients in a blender and puree. Serve very cold. Serves 4.

If you think cold soups are too much work, here's the world's fastest fruit soup from Marian Nicolas of Phoenix, Arizona.

COLD APRICOT SOUP

1/2 lb. fresh apricots
1 pint dry white California wine
1/4 cup sugar
Juice of one lemon

Pit 2 or 3 of the apricots and cut them into thin slices. Put aside. Pit the rest of the apricots and coarsely chop them. Put in blender and puree with the wine, sugar and lemon juice. Chill before using. Serve in deep glass bowls and garnish with the sliced apricots. Serve with plain cookies. Serves 4 to 6.

And if you are still in the cold-soup mood, Mrs. Ben Williams of Davis, California, thinks you will like this interesting version.

CONSOMME BURGUNDY

1 cup fresh squeezed lemon juice
2 cups California red wine
3 cups V-8 juice
4 cups consomme

Combine in a large saucepan. If it is to be served hot, heat to the boil. To serve cold, refrigerate 5 hours. Serves 8.

Mr. & Mrs. Harlow Gibbon of Spokane, Washington, serves this soup hot with a light lunch in the winter, and ice cold during the summer.

BUTTERMILK SOUP

2 eggs, well beaten
1/4 cup sugar or to taste
1 tsp. vanilla
juice and grated peel of 1 lemon
4 cups buttermilk
1 cup California white wine or Rose
Sliced fresh fruit (blueberries,
*   bananas, kiwi, strawberries)*

Combine eggs, sugar, vanilla, lemon juice and peel in small bowl and beat well. Whisk buttermilk and wine in large bowl until frothy. Slowly add egg mixture, whisking constantly. Cover and chill. Garnish with fruit. Serves 6.

If you like buttermilk and ice-cold soup, this is just your dish. It comes from Des Witkowski of Phoenix, Arizona.

SOPA VERDE

2 pkgs. fresh frozen peas
1 cup hot milk
1 cup chicken broth
2 egg yolks, well beaten
2 Tbs. butter
2 Tbs. flour
1/2 cup dry California white wine
1/2 tsp. chervil, crumbled
Salt and pepper to taste

Follow package instructions for cooking peas. Puree in blender or food processor. Set aside. Melt butter in heavy saucepan. When foaming, add flour and stir rapidly until well blended. Add hot milk and cook over low heat until thickened. Add broth, peas, egg yolks, chervil and seasonings. Blend, then add wine slowly and simmer for one minute. Garnish with mint leaves, if desired. Serves 6.

Here's another soup that will be easy on the budget and nice to the palate, according to Betty Frazier of Nokomis, Florida.

CHILLED CREAM OF AVOCADO SOUP

2 ripe avocados
1 cup chicken broth
1 1/2 cups heavy cream
1/2 cup California dry white wine
1 tsp. lemon juice
Salt and white pepper to taste
1/2 tsp. snipped dill

Halve, pit and peel avocados, and mash pulp. In a sauce pan, heat chicken broth until it is hot—remove from heat and stir in avocado. In a blender or a food processor fitted with the steel blade, puree the mixture. Transfer the puree to a large glass bowl and stir in heavy cream, wine, lemon juice and salt and pepper to taste. Cover the mixture and chill. Divide the soup among 4 chilled bowls and garnish with snipped dill. Serves 4.

Today avocados are available in almost every state of the Union, and there are many ways to fix and serve this tasty delight. Mrs. J. B. Brown in Costa Grande, Arizona, offers her friends avocados in this tangy way.

COLD SOUR CHERRY SOUP

3 cups cold water
1 cup sugar
1 cinnamon stick
4 cups pitted sour cherries or
    drained canned sour cherries
1 Tbs. arrowroot
1/4 cup heavy cream, chilled
1/4 cup dry California red wine,
    chilled

In a 2 quart saucepan, combine the water, sugar and cinnamon stick. Bring to a boil and add the cherries. Partially cover and simmer over low heat for 35 to 40 minutes if the cherries are fresh, or 10 minutes if they are canned. Remove the cinnamon stick. Mix the arrowroot and 2 tablespoons of cold water into a paste, then beat into the cooked cherries. Stirring constantly, bring the soup almost to a boil. Reduce the heat and simmer about 2 minutes, or until clear and slightly thickened. Pour into a shallow glass or stainless steel bowl, and refrigerate until chilled. Before serving, preferably in soup bowls that have been prechilled, stir in the cream and wine. Serves 6.

I really like this cool one from Sharnette Overeem of Wichita, Kansas.

OYSTER SOUP

1/4 cup butter
1/2 cup chopped celery
1/2 cup chopped onion
2 cloves garlic, crushed
2-8 oz. cans oysters
2 cups milk
1/2 cup heavy cream
1/2 tsp. salt
1/4 tsp. white pepper
1/2 cup chopped parsley
1/3 cup dry California Sherry
1/3 cup California white wine

Last year Phillipe Jeanty, chef de cuisine in the Napa Valley, showed me a new way to taste fresh oysters. He just drizzled a little sherry vinegar over them and ate them. They were exceptional. Denise Sutter of San Jose, California, uses oysters and sherry in her own exceptional way.

NAPA VALLEY CHEESE SOUP

1/2 cup carrots, diced
1/2 cup celery, diced
4 1/2 cups chicken stock
1/2 cup zucchini, diced
2 Tbs. butter
2 Tbs. onion, finely chopped
1/2 cup flour
1 cup sharp shredded Cheddar
  cheese
1/4 cup Parmesan cheese
10 drops hot sauce
Salt to taste
1/4 tsp. white pepper
1/2 cup California dry white wine
1 1/2 cups cream
parsley, chopped

Add carrots and celery to 1½ cups chicken stock in a 1 to 2 quart saucepan. Bring to boil; cover and simmer 10 minutes. Add zucchini and simmer another 5 minutes. Melt butter in 4 to 5 quart saucepan over medium heat; add onion and saute until transparent. Blend in flour and cook 5 to 7 minutes, stirring constantly, being careful not to brown. Slowly stir remaining cups chicken stock into flour mixture, whisking over low heat, until sauce thickens. Add cheeses and stir until melted. Season with hot sauce, salt, pepper, and wine. Stir in cream prior to serving. Garnish with chopped fresh parsley. Serves 6.

The English have always been fond of cheese soups. I think it is because they kept their houses quite cold and a thick hot cheese soup was just the thing to take the chills away. Janet Hill of Rodeo, California, thinks her cheese soup will hit your spot, too.

CALIFORNIA WINE SOUP JANINE

3½ cups white California wine
1 cup water
1/2 to 1 tsp. sugar, or to taste
1 stick whole cinnamon
1 to 2 inch slice lemon rind
4 egg yolks
2 Tbs. heavy sweet cream
1 tsp. flour
Salt to taste

In saucepan, combine water, 3 cups wine (refrigerate remaining 1/2 cup), sugar to taste, cinnamon stick and lemon rind. Bring to boil, turn down heat, simmer, skimming until clear. Remove from heat and strain. Return to saucepan and bring to a slow boil. In a bowl, beat egg yolks and cream, add flour, remaining cold wine and salt. Beat thoroughly until smooth. Stir quickly into boiling mixture, turn down heat immediately, beat with egg beaters to mix thoroughly. Serve at once in cups. Serves 6.

Over in Dumont, New Jersey, Mrs. Mildred K. Hornicek serves her friends this soup from first to last snowfall.

ESCARGOT SOUP

4 carrots
6 stalks celery
3 onions (large white)
8 shallots
4 cloves garlic, finely minced
1/4 lb. unsalted butter
2 cans escargot chopped fine
1/2 quart California Chardonnay
1 gallon of good consomme
1/2 tsp. fresh dill
1/2 tsp. thyme
1/2 tsp. basil
8 bay leaves
1/4 cup of dry California Sherry
2 quarts whipping cream
Dash of curry powder

Mince carrots, celery, onions, shallots and garlic and saute in unsalted butter until tender. In a separate sauce pan, bring to boil the white wine, escargot, consomme, then add seasonings. Strain, reserving escargot and seasonings. Thicken liquid with a very light roux, add vegetables and chopped escargot. Add Sherry to taste, mix in 2 quarts of heated cream and finish with a dash of curry powder. Serves 12.

Here is an unusual soup, seldom seen in restaurants, much less private homes; that didn't stop Barbara Morgan of Walnut Creek, California, from entering our competition.

BELGIAN ONION SOUP

4 large yellow onions, sliced thin
4 Tbs. butter
4 cups chicken stock
1 cup dry California white wine
Salt and pepper to taste
1/2 tsp. fines herbs
4 thick slices French bread, lightly
  toasted
4 to 6 oz. ripe Camembert cheese,
  softened

Saute onions in butter till soft and golden, but not brown. Add wine, chicken stock and fines herbs, salt and pepper to taste, and simmer gently for 20 minutes. Ladle the soup into four oven-proof bowls. Top each bowl with a slice of toasted French bread which has been spread with softened Camembert cheese. Place under the broiler and watch carefully. When the cheese turns just golden, the soup is ready to serve at once. Serves 4.

I am an onion soup freak. I have experimented for years trying to find the perfect onion soup. Barbara Karoff of Menlo Park, California, makes one that would be tops with any chef.

BROCCOLI WINE SOUP

1 bunch broccoli, saving 4 small
*   florets (chard, spinach,*
*   cauliflower or any favorite*
*   vegetable may be substituted)*
4 green onions
1 large apple
5 cups chicken broth
1 cup dry California white wine
1 tsp. fresh lemon juice
2 drops hot sauce
Salt and pepper to taste
1/4 cup fresh parsley
1 lemon, scored and sliced

Simmer vegetables in stock for 30 minutes. Add the reserved florets for the last minute, then remove and set aside for a garnish. Strain the vegetables from the stock and puree in a food processor or blender. Pour puree into the stock, add the wine, and stir until blended. Serve in four individual bowls and garnish with the reserved florets and a slice of lemon. Serves 4.

Wine and vegetables are fine together. The judges thought so too, because they awarded Nan Nielson of Eureka, California a certificate of appreciation for her broccoli and wine soup.

POTAGE CHAMPAGNE

3 cups shelled green peas
1 carrot
1 medium onion
1 oz. salt pork
1 bay leaf
1/8 tsp. each sage, chervil and
  thyme
3 cups chicken broth
1/2 cup California dry Sherry
1 tsp. lemon juice
1 cup heavy cream
1 split California Brut Champagne
  at room temperature

In a saucepan, combine peas, carrot, onion, salt pork, bay leaf, sage, chervil and thyme. Add water to cover. Cover and simmer until peas are very soft. Remove and discard the carrot, onion, bay leaf, and salt pork. Puree the mixture through a food mill into a bowl. Return the mixture to the saucepan. Stir in chicken broth, Sherry and lemon juice. Add salt and pepper to taste and bring the mixture to the boiling point. In a bowl, beat cream until it holds stiff peaks. Carefully fold it into the soup. Remove from heat and add Champagne. Serve immediately in heated bowls. Serves 6.

Lee McFerrin of Denver, Colorado won a certificate of appreciation by the judges for this unusual soup.

Pasta

PASTA

"Wine," said the old Italian, "is the only thing to drink with pasta."

"And to cook with, too," I said. He smiled, nodded his head and drained the glass of red wine in front of him.

It was noon. We were getting ready to feast in a small restaurant in Rome. The antipasto was already history; we were waiting for the Spaghetti Meretrice, a dish laced with garlic, anchovies, green and black olives, red peppers and a little red wine. There was salad, cheese and fruit afterward, and I walked away feeling very good.

Pasta is a versatile dish. It can be served as an appetizer course or a main course, depending upon the whim of the chef. And it can be married with many different ingredients.

SPAGHETTI BOURGUIGNON

1 lb. lean ground beef
1 medium onion, chopped
1/2 cup chopped green pepper
1 cup sliced mushrooms
2 cloves garlic, minced
1 can tomato paste
1-1 lb. can Italian style stewed
*   tomatoes*
1/2 cup California red wine
1 tsp. fennel
1 tsp. salt
1/4 tsp. black pepper
1 tsp. crushed basil
1/2 tsp. oregano
12 oz. long spaghetti, cooked and
*   drained*

Brown beef, add garlic, onion, pepper and mushrooms; cook until tender. Add remaining ingredients except spaghetti. Simmer uncovered 1/2 hour; cover and simmer 20 minutes. Add more wine as sauce thickens. Serve over hot spaghetti. Serves 6.

I am not sure why Janet Creager of Spokane, Washington, calls her dish Spaghetti Bourguignon, but I suspect it is because she uses a California red wine in the recipe. Be that as it may, you will enjoy her dish.

SUMMER SPAGHETTI ROMA

*1/4 lb. lean, thick-sliced bacon, cut
  into squares*
2 Tbs. olive oil
1 cup sweet onion, coarsely cubed
1/4 cup water
1/4 tsp. dried flaked red pepper
*1/2 tsp. garlic powder (or more, to
  taste)*
*4 or 5 medium-sized ripe tomatoes,
  peeled and cut into chunks*
1/2 cup California dry white wine
1 tsp. dried sweet basil
Salt to taste
*Grated Romano, Pecorino or
  Parmesan cheese*
3/4 to 1 lb. thin spaghetti

Saute bacon chunks until golden, but not entirely crisp. Remove from pan and drain, leaving 2 Tbs. bacon drippings. Add olive oil, onion and water; simmer 3 minutes. Add wine, garlic and tomatoes. Add bacon and red pepper. Cook 3 minutes. Add sweet basil; taste for salt and add if needed. (A light touch here, please. Cheese added later will add salt.) Cook about 5 more minutes, or until slightly blended—tomatoes should remain in chunks and sauce should be a bit liquid. Pour sauce over cooked and drained spaghetti. Reheat in serving casserole, tossing with 1/2 to 3/4 cup grated cheese. Serves 4.

I have never spent a summer in Rome, but people who have say that, despite the tourists, Rome can be fun. The best times are late in the afternoon, after the shops have re-opened and the life of Rome seems to catch its second wind. Romans eat lean in the hot summer months, and Betty Frazier of Nokomis, Florida, shows us how to eat like the Romans.

SAN FRANCISCO CRABMEAT SPAGHETTI

1 Tbs. oil
1 large white onion, chopped
4 large stalks celery
1 Tbs. parsley, chopped
1/4 tsp. garlic powder
1-16 oz. can of tomatoes
1-8 oz. can of tomato sauce
3/4 cup water
3/4 cup California white wine
1 lb. crab meat
Spaghetti for five
1 cup Parmesan cheese

Heat oil in skillet. Add onion and celery and brown lightly. Add parsley, garlic powder, tomatoes, tomato sauce, water and wine. Simmer 30 minutes. Add crabmeat and heat. Cook spaghetti according to package instructions and mix with sauce. Put in baking dish and cover with Parmesan cheese. Bake until bubbly. Serves 5.

This terrific spaghetti variation comes from Mrs. R. Kinyon of N. Ogden, Utah.

BAKED SPAGHETTI

1½ lbs. ground beef
1 medium onion, minced
1 clove garlic, mashed or chopped
 fine
1/4 cup oil
3-8 oz. cans tomato sauce
1 cup California red wine
1 tsp. dried Italian herbs
1/2 tsp. dried parsley
1 Tbs. sugar
1/2 tsp. salt
1/4 tsp. pepper
1/2 lb. spaghetti, broken in 2 inch
 lengths
1 1/2 cups grated American
 cheese—medium sharp or sharp

Saute meat, onion and garlic in heated oil. Add tomato sauce, wine, herbs, parsley, sugar, salt and pepper. Simmer, covered, 1 hour, stirring occasionally. Cook spaghetti according to package directions; drain, add spaghetti and 1/2 cup cheese to sauce. Turn into 3 quart casserole; sprinkle with remaining 1 cup cheese. (If made ahead, do not sprinkle cheese on top until ready to bake.) Cover; bake in a moderately slow oven 325 degrees for 45 minutes. Uncover, bake 30 minutes longer. Serves 6.

What is the world's tastiest spaghetti? Well, just ask Hazel Mower of Garden Grove, California, and she'll give you this recipe.

Chicken

CHICKEN

You are not going to believe this, but the ancestor of all chickens is the pheasant. Some 6,000 years ago, man began to tame a pheasant called the Red Jungle Fowl and today we have the barnyard chicken (if we are lucky) and the domesticated force-fed push-a-bell-and-they-eat fowl.

My grandmother Hebert raised barnyard chickens. I can still see her in the backyard of her small home in Raceland, Louisiana. She would gather up her apron, fill it with dried corn, descend the few stairs to her backyard where the chickens roamed freely, and chant "Here chick-chick-chick-chick-chick-chick; Here chick-chick-chick-chick-chick." They would scramble toward her as she scattered handfuls of corn and gobble it up as if it was the best food in the world. But that was all they were fed, except water. They had to scratch the dirt for anything else in their diets.

I can still taste those barnyard chickens my grandmother raised. I helped her clean them and watched with some degree of awe how she cooked them. Nothing has ever tasted so good.

CALIFORNIA SHERRY-SOY MARINADE

1 cup soy sauce
1 cup California dry Sherry
3 cloves garlic
2 Tbs. diced ginger root
4 Tbs. honey
1-3 lb. chicken, cut up

Pulverize garlic and ginger with pestle or wooden spoon. Add soy sauce, honey and Sherry. Shake well in quart jar or refrigerator container and use as needed. Chicken should be marinated 3 hours.

One of the best ways to fix chicken is using a marinade. Betty B. Anderson of Avon, Connecticut, offers this flavorful marinade combining California Sherry and soy sauce.

CHICKEN SHERRY MARINADE

1-3 lb. chicken fryer, cut up into
parts
1/2 cup soy sauce
1/2 cup white vinegar
1/2 cup California dry Sherry
2 cloves garlic, crushed
3 slices of fresh ginger
3 Tbs. peanut oil

Marinate chicken overnight in everything except the peanut oil. Next day, heat peanut oil in large frying pan and saute chicken until brown and crisp on the outside. Add the marinade juice and continue cooking until chicken is cooked through, about 45 minutes. Best served over rice. Serves 4.

Several thousand miles away in San Francisco, Eliska B. Meyers also makes a special chicken marinade.

CALIFORNIA WHITE WINE
CHICKEN MARINADE

1 cup California white wine
1/2 cup lemon juice
1 cup salad oil
1 Tbs. sugar
1 Tbs. salt
1 cup finely chopped onion
2 cloves garlic, mashed
1/8 tsp. thyme
1/8 tsp. curry powder
1 Tbs. paprika
Few drops Tabasco sauce
1-3 lb. chicken, cut up

Combine all ingredients. Stir to blend. Marinate cut-up chicken parts in the sauce for 4 or 5 hours or as long as 24 hours in the refrigerator. Grill until chicken is tender, basting often with the sauce. Serves 6.

And this third marinade with a touch of Indian spicing is from Mary J. Adams of Saratoga, California.

LIMEHOUSE CHICKEN

6 chicken breasts
1 lime
1/3 cup flour
1 1/2 tsp. salt
1 Tbs. paprika
1/4 cup cooking oil
2 Tbs. brown sugar
1/2 cup chicken broth
1/2 cup California white wine
2 sprigs fresh mint, chopped
For garnish: 1 avocado, 1 lime,
*   and sprigs of fresh mint*

Preheat oven to 375 degrees. Wash chicken and pat dry. Grate peel from lime and set aside. Squeeze lime juice over chicken pieces and shake in a bag containing flour, salt and paprika. Heat oil in heavy skillet (with cover) and brown chicken on all sides. Pour off all the oil and arrange chicken in skillet in a single layer. Combine lime peel and brown sugar. Sprinkle over chicken. Add broth and wine. Place chopped mint on top. Bake, covered, at 375 degrees for 45 minutes. Garnish with lime wedges, avocado slices, and fresh mint. Serves 4.

The lime has always been a part of gourmet cookery. It imparts a special flavor all its own and can lift a dish to new heights. Jerry B. Shannon of Ropesville, Texas, offers this version.

HAMPTON'S CHICKEN BREASTS

4 chicken breasts, boned and
    skinned
4 Tbs. butter
1 cup finely chopped onion
4 Tbs. flour
1 cup California white wine
1 13 oz. can chicken broth
1 cup milk
1-8 oz. package noodles, cooked and
    drained

Season chicken breasts with salt and pepper. Melt butter and saute chicken 2 minutes; add onions and stir. Cover and cook 8 to 10 minutes. Remove chicken. Sprinkle flour over onions and stir in wine and broth. Bring to a boil. Add milk and simmer 5 minutes. Return chicken for 5 minutes. Serves 4.

My mother often made a chicken and spaghetti dish, using the whole chicken cut up in parts. But Mel Hampton in Dallas, Texas, may have a better version.

CHICKEN WITH LEMON & GARLIC

20-25 cloves garlic
2 cups chicken stock
1 chicken, cut up
Salt and pepper
Butter
1 lemon
2 Tbs. butter
2 Tbs. flour
1/2 cup dry white California wine

Peel garlic, parboil for 5 minutes. Drain and poach in chicken stock for 40 minutes with cover on. Salt and pepper chicken. Heat butter and brown chicken thoroughly. Place in a casserole with a lid. Drain poached garlic, saving chicken stock. Scatter drained garlic on top of chicken in casserole. Peel the lemon, removing all of the white skin. Slice in rounds, remove seeds and scatter on top of chicken and garlic.

  Sauce: Make a roux by melting the butter, adding the flour and whisking and cooking for a couple of seconds—do not brown. Add wine and stock. Whisk until smooth and simmer for 15 minutes. Pour sauce over chicken, cover and bake for 40 to 45 minutes at 375 degrees. Correct seasonings. Serves 4 to 6.

Whatever you do, do not let this next recipe scare you. There are many dishes in various cuisines that call for what we Americans seem to think is a lot of garlic. Slow cooking of garlic reduces its pungency and makes it a welcome treat, as Julie Hicks of Fresno, California, shows us.

PARTY CHICKEN CACCIATORE

3 chicken breasts, halved, skinned
and boned
2 Tbs. each oil and butter
2 green peppers, seeded and chopped
1/2 pound fresh mushrooms, sliced
1 medium onion, chopped
2 cloves garlic, pressed
2/3 cup California red wine
2/3 cup chicken broth
1 6 oz. can tomato paste
1 tsp. salt
1/4 tsp. each oregano, basil, thyme
and pepper
8 ounces pasta, cooked and drained
Grated Parmesan cheese

Heat oil and butter in large skillet over medium-high heat. Cut chicken breasts into large bite-sized pieces. Add to skillet and cook, turning, until browned on all sides. Remove from pan and reserve. Add peppers, mushrooms, onion and garlic to skillet; reduce heat to medium. Cook, stirring often, until onion is limp. Add wine, broth, tomato paste and seasonings; stir until well mixed. Bring to a boil, reduce heat, cover and simmer 35 minutes, stirring occasionally. Return chicken pieces (plus any accumulation of juices) to skillet; continue to simmer, covered, about 20 minutes longer, until chicken is fork-tender. Place hot, cooked pasta on heated platter; top with chicken and sauce. Sprinkle on small amount of grated parmesan. Serves 5.

There must be as many recipes for Chicken Cacciatore as there are Italians in Italy. That may be a slight exaggeration, but there are plenty of variations upon variations. Shirley DeSantis of Bethlehem, Pennsylvania, shares her family recipe with us.

LAYERED CHICKEN ASPARAGUS

3 cups medium noodles
3 Tbs. butter or margarine
1/2 lb. mushrooms, sliced
1/2 cup chopped celery
1-1 lb. can tomatoes, cut up
1-15 ounce can tomato sauce
1/2 cup California Rosé
1/2 tsp. sugar
1/2 tsp. salt
1/2 tsp. garlic salt
1-8 ounce package cream cheese,
*   softened*
1/2 cup sour cream
3 Tbs. milk
2 Tbs. chopped onion
Dash of nutmeg
1 cup large-chunked cooked
*   chicken*
2 8-ounce packages frozen cut
*   asparagus, cooked and drained*
1/2 cup shredded, jack cheese

Cook noodles in boiling salted water until tender, about 10 minutes; drain and set aside. Melt butter in large skillet; add mushrooms and celery. Cook over low heat until soft, about 10 minutes. Add tomatoes, tomato sauce, wine, sugar, salt and garlic salt: simmer another 10 minutes. Spoon a little sauce into bottom of greased 12x8x2 baking dish. Arrange cooked noodles in sauce; add a little more sauce. Stir together cream cheese, sour cream, milk, onion and nutmeg. Layer half of cream cheese mixture over mixture in baking dish; then all of the asparagus, then the chicken. Add remaining wine sauce. Cover and bake in 350 degree oven for 40 minutes or until bubbly. Uncover and spread remaining cream cheese mixture on top; sprinkle with jack cheese. Bake 10 minutes more or until cheese melts. Serves 6.

If you are looking for a buffet surprise, I recommend this dish from Norma Jean Coppenbarger of Sacramento, California.

BAKED CHICKEN IN MICROWAVE

1 whole chicken or 4 chicken breasts
2 Tbs. chopped onions
1 Tbs. parsley flakes
1/2 tsp. celery salt
1 tsp. oregano
2 Tbs. butter
Paprika
1/2 cup fresh sliced mushrooms
1½ cups California white wine

Wash and remove excess fat from chicken. Place chicken in covered casserole dish and pierce chicken in legs and breast with fork. Add all the ingredients but the mushrooms. Microwave on High for 10 minutes, covered. Remove cover and add mushrooms. Sprinkle paprika over chicken. Return to oven and Microwave 6 minutes on high. Remove and let stand covered for 10 minutes. Test leg for doneness. Serves 4.

The microwave oven is here to stay. Just what its total use will be in later years has yet to be determined. But Mrs. John W. Deeds of Sarasota, Florida, has developed this recipe using the magic of microwave cooking.

CHICKEN SAUTE WITH RASPBERRY VINEGAR

4 large split chicken breasts,
* skinned and boned*
Salt and freshly ground white
* pepper*
1 Tbs. butter
1 tsp. dried tarragon or 1 1/2 tsp.
* fresh, minced*
1 shallot, minced
1 clove garlic, pressed
1/3 cup dry California white wine
1½ tsp. raspberry vinegar
1 tomato peeled, seeded and coarsly
* chopped*
1/3 cup heavy cream

Pound chicken breasts between sheets of waxed paper to even thickness. Season with salt and pepper. Saute chicken in butter, turning to brown on both sides. Add tarragon, shallots, garlic and wine. Cover and simmer 15 minutes. Transfer chicken to heated platter and keep warm. Add vinegar to pan juices and reduce by 1/2. Scrape pan to deglaze. Add tomato and heat through. Pour in cream and reduce slightly to form slightly thickened sauce. Spoon over the chicken and serve at once. Serves 4.

Cooking with flavored vinegars seems to be all the rage right now. Few people know that vinegars—plain, wine based or fruit flavored—have been in the kitchen for some 1,000 years. Barbara Karoff of Menlo Park, California, uses raspberry vinegar for her chicken, and it works beautifully.

CHICKEN IN WINE

---

2 1/2 lb. fryer chicken, cut up
1/2 cup all purpose flour
1 tsp. salt
1/4 tsp. pepper
8 slices bacon
8 small onions
8 oz. mushrooms—sliced
4 carrots, cut in halves
1 cup chicken broth
1 cup dry California red wine
1 clove garlic, crushed
Snipped parsley

Cut chicken in pieces, cut each breast half into halves. Mix flour, salt and pepper. Coat chicken with flour mixture. Fry bacon in skillet until crisp. Drain. Cook chicken in hot bacon fat until brown. Set chicken aside. Add onions and mushrooms. Cook and stir until mushrooms are tender. Drain fat from skillet. Crumble bacon and stir into vegetables with remaining ingredients, cover and simmer until thickest parts of chicken are done (about 35 minutes). Skim off excess fat, sprinkle chicken with snipped parsley, if desired.

Mrs. R. T. Conley of Sarasota, Florida, has created this chicken-and-red-wine dish, which she likes to serve her friends.

POLLOS BORRACHOS

2-3 lb. chickens, quartered
pepper, freshly grated
2 cloves garlic, minced
Vegetable oil
3 medium onions, thickly sliced
1/3 cup fresh parsley, chopped
2 Tbs. sesame seeds
1 cinnamon stick, broken into
*   small pieces*
1 bay leaf
1/4 tsp. whole cloves
1 cup California Gewurztraminer
1 Tbs. vinegar (cider or white)
16 (or more) small stuffed green
*   olives*
1 tsp. cornstarch dissolved in small
*   amount cold water*
Additional chopped fresh parsley
*   for garnish*

About 1 hour before serving, sprinkle chicken with pepper and garlic. Heat oil in Dutch oven. Saute onions, parsley, and sesame seeds until onions are soft (about 5 minutes). Add chicken and cook over medium heat until light brown on all sides. Stir in cinnamon, bay leaf, and cloves and cook 1 to 2 minutes. Add wine, vinegar, and olives and simmer, covered, 30 to 45 minutes, or until chicken is cooked and tender. Remove chicken to warm platter. Use slotted spoon to remove all solids from pot and spread evenly over chicken pieces. Keep warm. Add cornstarch mixed with water to pan juices, and heat until juices thicken. Serve sauce alongside chicken or pour directly over chicken. Top chicken with more chopped fresh parsley before serving. Serves 6.

Wine and chicken are almost the perfect cooking partners. And the most famous dish is red wine with chicken, onions, bits of bacon or salt pork, a bay leaf and a good bottle of California wine. This unusual variation on that dish comes from Louise May of New York.

FisH

F I S H

Fish and wine have a natural affinity. In their subtlety and great diversity, the taste of each has the ability to complement the other in ways as surprising as they are pleasing.

When matching fish and wine, look out for fish which are naturally oily. The oil lingers on the taste buds, and makes it difficult to taste and appreciate any wine. For example, trout has an oil-rich gray-black streak running down the back, which should be removed before serving. Other oily fish include herring, mackerel, catfish, tuna, swordfish, and salmon.

Whenever possible, use fresh fish. Unfortunately, fresh fish is not available in many parts of the country. However, new quick-freezing methods have greatly improved the flavor and texture of frozen fish in recent years, making them an excellent alternative if fresh is not available.

SPANISH FISH

2/3 cup finely chopped onion
2/3 cup finely chopped green pepper
2 Tbs. oil
1/2 cup California white wine
1-15 oz. can tomato sauce
1 bay leaf
1 tsp. garlic salt
1/4 tsp. oregano
1/2 tsp. hot pepper sauce
1 lb. fish fillets (turbot is good)

Cook onion and pepper in oil until tender. Add wine, tomato sauce, bay leaf, garlic salt, oregano and hot pepper sauce. Simmer for 10 minutes. While simmering, separate fish into 4 portions. Add fish to simmered sauce. Cover and simmer for 20 minutes, or until fish flakes when pricked with fork. Serves 4.

Over in Charlottesville, Virginia, a lot of people are delighted with Lois Gasparro's Spanish fish fillets.

HALIBUT TERIYAKI

1 1/2 lbs. of halibut fillets
1/2 cup California white wine
2 Tbs. vegetable oil
3 Tbs. soy sauce
1/2 tsp. dry mustard
1/2 tsp. ground ginger
1/4 tsp. garlic powder
2 tsp. parsley flakes

Place fillets in a plastic bag. Combine wine, oil, soy sauce, mustard, ginger, garlic powder and parsley flakes; pour into bag with fillets. Close bag tightly, place in a shallow dish. Allow fish to marinate about 2 hours, turning bag several times. Drain fillets, reserving marinade. Broil 5 minutes; brush with marinade. Broil 1 minute longer, turn. Brush with marinade; broil 5 minutes, or until fish is brown and flakes easily with a fork. Serves 4.

I salute fish-fillet lover Reba Slotkin of Sarasota, Florida, who serves it Japanese style.

TROUT IN WHITE WINE

6 mountain trout (about 1 1/2 lbs.
  each), boned
Salt and pepper
1/2 cup finely chopped onion
1/4 cup minced parsley
2 Tbs. butter
1½ cups California white wine
lemon slices
parsley sprigs
Beurre blanc (recipe follows)

Season fish inside and out with salt and pepper. Saute onion and minced parsley in butter, stuff into fish. Place in greased shallow baking pan. Add enough wine to cover bottom of pan. Bake at 400 degrees 10 minutes; baste with remaining wine, reduce heat to 300 degrees and cook 15 minutes or until fish is tender. Serve on hot platter and garnish with lemon slices and parsley. Accompany with beurre blanc. Serves 6.

BEURRE BLANC

2 shallots, chopped fine
3 Tbs. white wine vinegar
3 Tbs. dry California white wine
3/4 cup butter at room temperature

Add shallots to vinegar and wine and cook until they are completely soft and liquid is reduced to 1 Tablespoon. Cool. Add butter, about 2 Tablespoons at a time, cooking over low heat and beating continuously with a wire whisk until sauce is the consistency of thick cream.

One of the best-tasting fish is trout. Marian Nicolaus of Phoenix, Arizona, likes to cook it in California white wine and then top the dish with a special white butter sauce.

SNAPPER MEUNIERE

2 red snapper fillets
4 Tbs. butter
1 Tbs. flour
Juice of 1 lemon
1/2 cup California white wine
1 Tbs. white vinegar
1 Tbs. capers
Salt and pepper to taste

Rinse snapper and pat dry. Melt butter in frying pan over medium heat and saute fish until cooked through, about 2 to 3 minutes on each side. Place on heated serving dish and keep warm. Add flour to remaining butter and juices in pan and stir until evenly combined and thickened. Add lemon juice, wine, vinegar and capers and heat through till boiling. Simmer 1 to 2 minutes, add salt and pepper to taste. Pour sauce over fish and serve, immediately. Serves 2.

Another great-tasting fish is red snapper. Californians are lucky to have a plentiful supply of red snapper. However, Eliska B. Meyers of San Francisco wouldn't mind if you substituted another firm-fleshed fish.

POOR MAN'S LOBSTER NEWBURG

2 cups cubed codfish
3 Tbs. butter or margarine
1/2 cup California dry Sherry
1 1/2 cups cream
3 egg yolks
1/4 tsp. salt
1/8 tsp. pepper
1 tsp. paprika
Dash cayenne
6 baked patty shells (if desired)

Saute cod in butter five minutes. Add Sherry; simmer until wine is almost reduced. Beat cream with yolks, salt, pepper, paprika and cayenne. Add to cod, stirring constantly until thickened. Do not boil. Spoon into patty shells, if desired. Serves 6.

The price of lobster today is extraordinarily high. That's because they are in great demand but take about seven years to reach catchable size. Gloria T. Bove of Bethlehem, Pennsylvania, has solved the problem this way.

BABY CLAMS CACCIUCCO

1/4 cup olive oil
2 Tbs. parsley chopped fine, fresh
   Italian preferred
1 medium size onion, chopped
   small
4 anchovy fillets, minced or cut up
1 clove garlic, minced
1/2 cup celery chopped
1 medium size carrot chopped
1/2 bell green pepper chopped
3 medium sized potatoes cut in
   cubes, small
1 Tbs. tomato paste
2 cups chopped tomatoes, fresh
   or canned
1 cup California white wine
2 cups boiling water
1/4 tsp. each thyme and oregano
1 bay leaf
1 hot red chili pepper or 1/2 tsp.
   chili flakes
Ground pepper and salt to taste
1-10 oz. can baby clams, using
   liquid too
Toasted or fried Italian bread
Chopped parsley for garnish

Heat oil in heavy pot. Saute the parsley, onion, anchovies and garlic. Stir and heat until lightly golden but not brown. Add celery, carrots, green pepper and herbs. Cook 3 more minutes. Add tomatoes, liquids, tomato paste, and wine. Mix well. Add potatoes. Keep on low simmer for 20 minutes. Add the can of clams, heat 5 more minutes to blend flavors. Serve in bowls containing Italian bread and sprinkle parsley on top. Serves 4 to 6.

Mrs. Libia Foglesong of San Bruno, California, entered her clam recipe in the soup category. Well, Mrs. Foglesong, we tasted it and it is a meal in itself, so we placed it in the fish division.

COQUILLES ST. JACQUES

3 Tbs. butter
2 pints fresh scallops
Salt and pepper to taste
2 Tbs. finely chopped shallots, or
*   onions*
2 cups sliced fresh mushrooms
10 cherry tomatoes, or 12 pieces
*   tomatoes, quartered*
1/4 cup California white wine
1 cup heavy cream
1 Tbs. finely chopped parsley

Heat 2 Tablespoons butter in one large skillet or two medium size skillets. When butter is quite hot and before it browns, add the scallops. Cook over high heat, shaking the skillet and stirring. Sprinkle with salt and pepper. Cook one or two minutes, until lightly golden. The less cooking time the better. Using a slotted spoon, remove the scallops and keep them warm. To the skillet add the shallots and cook briefly. Add the mushrooms and tomatoes and cook, stirring often, about one minute. Add the wine and reduce the liquid by half. Add the cream, salt and pepper to taste. Cook down over high heat about three minutes. Add the scallops. Swirl in the remaining tablespoon of butter. Sprinkle with chopped parsley. Serve with rice. Serves 4.

Unlike its close relatives the mussel, oyster and clam, scallops are lively fellows that rarely attach themselves to a single place. They are found throughout the world. Here's how Mrs. Marie L. Settimo of Springfield, New Jersey, likes to serve them.

SEA SCALLOPS A LA PARISIENNE

1 1/2 lbs. scallops
1 1/2 cups California white wine
1/2 tsp. salt
1/4 tsp. paprika
3 Tbs. butter
2 Tbs. flour
1 cup milk
1/2 cup coarsely chopped fresh
  mushrooms
2 Tbs. grated Swiss cheese
2 Tbs. dry bread crumbs

In a saucepan combine scallops, wine, salt and paprika and simmer gently for 5 minutes. Drain scallops, saving cooking liquid. Cut scallops into four pieces. In a heavy saucepan heat butter and add the flour. Stir in cooking liquid and milk to make a sauce. Simmer 3 minutes, stirring all the time. Add to the sauce the scallops and mushrooms. Bring mixture to a boil and immediately remove it from the fire. Stir in the cheese, mixing well. Fill buttered shells or individual casseroles with the mixture. Sprinkle over with the bread crumbs. Dot with additional little bits of butter. Broil until top is golden brown. Serves 4.

Over in Austin, Texas Maruja Hathaway gives scallops an international flavor.

SHRIMP SOUFFLE

6 slices white bread
1 1/4 lb. cooked medium or small
*   shrimp*
1/2 lb. old English cheese
1/4 cup butter, melted
1/2 tsp. dry mustard
3 whole eggs, beaten
1/4 cup dry California white wine
1 pint milk
Salt to taste

Break or cut bread into pieces—quarter size. Break or cut cheese into bite size pieces and separate. Grease 2 quart casserole. Arrange shrimp, bread and cheese in several layers. Pour butter over this. Then pour wine over this. Beat eggs. Add mustard and salt, then milk. Pour this over other ingredients in casserole. Let stand a minimum of 3 hours, preferrably overnight, in refrigerator, covered. Bake covered at 350 degrees for one hour. Serves 6.

The first shrimp I ever tasted came from the Gulf of Mexico off the coast of Louisiana. I had two uncles who were shrimpmen. They left early in the morning and returned late at night with shrimp which had never seen ice. We used to boil them while they were still alive and those were the best-tasting shrimp in the whole world. Today, we are forced to eat frozen shrimp because again, the demand exceeds the supply. Lynn Riley in Walnut Creek, California, shares her specialty.

SHRIMPS IN A SHELL

4 Tbs. butter
3 Tbs. flour
1 1/2 cups milk
1 tsp. salt
Dash of white pepper
Dash paprika
1/3 cup California white wine
1 lb. shrimp, shelled and cooked
5 Tbs. Parmesan cheese, grated

Melt butter in saucepan, stir in flour. Add milk slowly. Cook slowly, stirring constantly until thickened. Stir in salt, pepper, paprika and wine. Simmer five minutes. Add shrimps, simmer two minutes. Pour into five baking shells: sprinkle each shell with one teaspoonful of grated cheese. Put under broiler, 3 to 4 inches from heat. Broil until cheese turns brown. Serves 5.

And James E. Alvar of Kingman, Arizona, likes his shrimp in the shell—sort of.

TUNA SCRAMBLE

2 medium white boiling onions,
*   chopped*
3 or 4 stalks celery, chopped
1/4 of large bell pepper, chopped
1 or 2 cloves garlic, minced
2 Tbs. oil drained from tuna
1-9 oz. can tuna, drained
1 tsp. chicken bouillon granules
1/2 cup California dry Sherry
1/2 cup milk
1 Tbs. cornstarch
1/2 tsp. dried dill leaves
1/4 tsp. dried thyme
1 egg, beaten
1 tomato, cut in 6 wedges

Saute first 5 ingredients until just tender; add tuna. Sprinkle in bouillon granules.
Add Sherry and stir. Mix cornstarch and milk, add to tuna mixture. Cook gently
until slightly thickened. Add herbs and beaten egg, stir, add tomato and cook
gently, covered, about 2 minutes longer. Serves 2 to 3.

Tuna is probably one of the most popular fishes in the world. Lois B. Watt of
Stanford, California, serves it this way.

RAGOUT OF SEAFOOD AU VIN ROUGE

2 red onions sliced paper thin
6 cloves garlic diced
2 Tbs. olive oil
1/2 tsp. dill
1½ cups light-bodied California red
  wine (Gamay or Rosé)
1 Tbs. soy sauce
2 lbs. fresh seafood in 2 ounce
  pieces (snapper, shrimp, tuna,
  sea bass, monkfish, etc.)
1 cup snowpeas

Saute onions, garlic in olive oil until translucent. Add dill, wine and soy sauce. Bring to a boil, add seafood and poach until barely done. Add snowpeas in last minute of poaching. Serve in a bowl over rice or pasta. Serves 4.

John Bolton, executive chef of the Club Snowbird, in Snowbird, Utah, knows the value of fresh fish, and suggests this American version of a French fish ragout.

SHERRIED OYSTERS BORDESSA

2 jars fresh oysters
1 egg, beaten
1 cup seasoned bread crumbs,
  mixed with 2 Tbs. flour
3 Tbs. butter
3 cloves garlic, minced
1 medium onion, diced
1 lb. fresh mushrooms, sliced
1 bunch green onions, chopped
2 Tbs. garlic salt
1 cup dry California Sherry

Drain oysters in colander, rinse in cold water. In pie plate, beat egg. Add oysters and toss gently until well coated. Then, carefully roll oysters in bread crumbs. Allow to dry 10 minutes. In frying pan melt butter. Add garlic, onions and mushrooms. Lightly saute over low heat. Remove from pan, leaving butter. Set aside. Turn heat to medium and fry oysters in butter until golden brown. Place sauteed mushroom mixture over oysters. Sprinkle garlic salt over mushrooms then pour Sherry over entire ingredients in pan. Cover with lid. Simmer for 10 minutes over medium heat. Remove from heat and serve over a bed of steamed rice. Garnish with lemon wedges. Serves 6.

Vicki Bordessa of Santa Rosa, California, likes her oysters fresh for her special Sherry recipe.

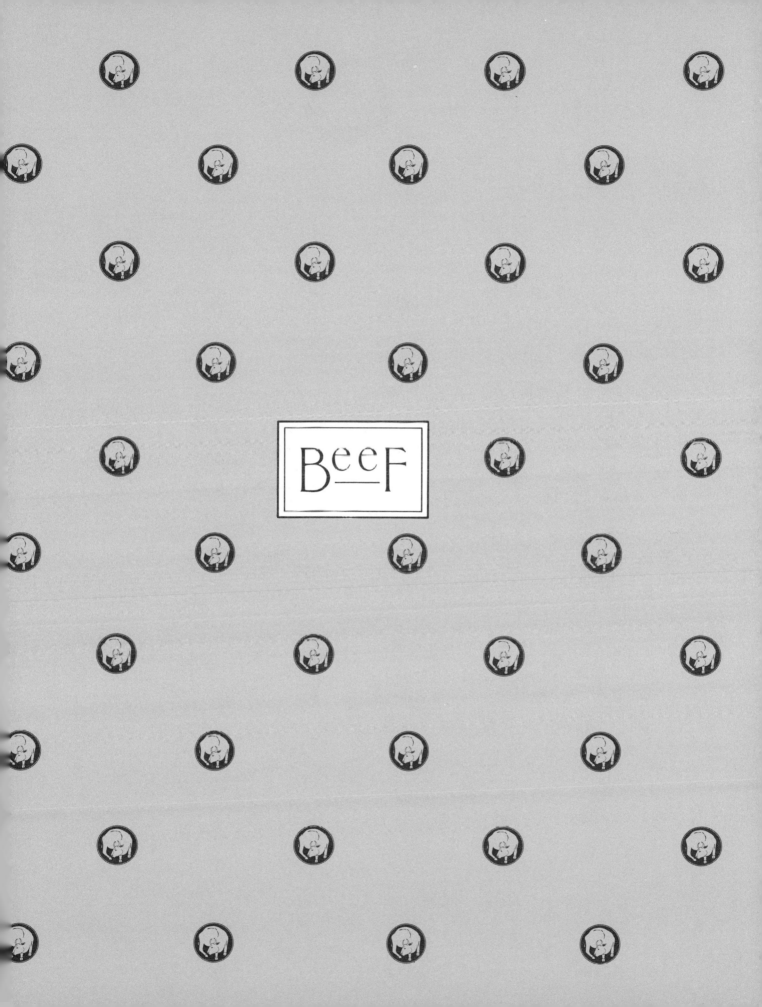

BEEF

No matter how you prefer it, beef is still one of man's favorite meats.

A decade ago, if the Wine Institute had held a similar competition, most of the recipes it would have received would have been on grilling or barbecuing beef. Today, the recipes are calling for innovative preparation and less expensive cuts of beef, reflecting a major shift in the eating habits of many Americans.

Veal has always been a favorite entree in the world of cuisine. Its popularity in the United States has grown so fast in the past 25 years that today there are several firms that specialize in raising veal.

PUMPKIN BEEF STEW

2 lbs. lean beef cut into one inch
  cubes
1 cup flour
1/2 tsp. salt
1 tsp. pepper
6 Tbs. oil
1/2 cup California brandy
1 cup coarsely chopped onion
1 cup chopped green pepper
3 minced garlic cloves
3 cups beef stock
1 cup California dry Sherry or dry
  red wine
3 tomatoes, chopped
2 bay leaves
1/2 tsp. oregano
1 1/2 lbs. potatoes, cubed
1 lb. sweet potatoes, sliced thick
1 lb. zucchini, sliced thick
3 ears fresh corn cut into 1-inch
  thick rounds*
16 dried, pitted prunes
1-10 to 12 lb. pumpkin, scrubbed
1/2 cup butter
1 cup brown sugar
4 Tbs. cinnamon

Recipe continued next page . . .

(*Note: A sharp cleaver is helpful to slice through the corn cob. Alternatively, the corn may be used off the cob; this is not as decorative, but is much easier to prepare and to eat.)

Toss the beef cubes in a mixture of the flour, salt and pepper to coat; shake off the excess flour. In small batches, brown the cubes on all sides in 4 Tbs. of oil in a 4 to 5 quart pan. Add the brandy, stir briefly. Transfer the meat and juices to a platter and set aside. In the same pan, combine remaining oil, onions, green pepper and garlic and cook, stirring, until vegetables are slightly soft and lightly browned. Pour in beef stock and wine. Bring mixture to a boil, scraping up any browned bits clinging to the pan. Return the meat and juices to the pan. Stir in tomatoes, bay leaf and oregano. Cover, reduce heat to low and simmer for 15 minutes. Add potatoes, and cook, covered, for 15 minutes. Stir in corn and cook, covered, 5 minutes. Add zucchini and prunes and cook, covered for 3 minutes. Simmer over very low heat for at least 1 hour while preparing pumpkin. Preheat the oven to 375 degrees. Slice the pumpkin across about four inches down from the stem to form a lid about six inches in diameter. Scrape the seeds and stringy fiber from the lid and the shell. Melt the butter and brush the inside of the pumpkin with it. Sprinkle the shell with the sugar and cinnamon. Put on the lid, place the pumpkin in a well-greased roasting pan and bake for about 45 minutes. Watch carefully toward the end of the baking time; the pumpkin should be firm enough to hold the stew without collapsing and the pulp should still be somewhat firm when pierced with a fork. Pour the juices that have accumulated in the pumpkin into the stew and blend well. Place the stew into the pumpkin and bake for 15 minutes. To serve, ladle the stew into bowls, scraping up some pumpkin pulp for each serving. Both the pumpkin and the stew may be prepared in advance. If so, reheat both before adding the stew to the pumpkin for the final 15 minute baking period. Serves 8 to 10.

Here's the Grand Prize winner as selected by the panel of judges. The top prize went to Karen Harmatiuk of Santa Clara, California.

BIG GUY'S BEEF STEW

2 lbs. stewing beef, cubed
1 egg, beaten
Dried bread crumbs
Cooking oil
4 Tbs. olive oil
2 Tbs. sweet butter
4 cloves garlic, minced
6 oz. can tomato paste
1 cup California red wine
2-16 oz. cans stewed tomatoes
3 bay leaves
1 tsp. basil
1 tsp. oregano
1 tsp. salt
1 tsp. fresh ground pepper
5 medium carrots, chunked
1 lb. white onions, peeled, chunked
6 medium potatoes, pared and
   cubed
1-10 oz. package frozen peas,
   thawed
Fresh parsley

Dip beef cubes in beaten egg; then coat cubes with bread crumbs. Heat cooking oil in skillet and then brown beef cubes on all sides. In 4 quart Dutch oven, heat olive oil and butter. Lightly saute garlic and then add tomato paste. Simmer for five minutes. Add wine and simmer for five minutes. Add stewed tomatoes, browned beef, bay leaves, basil, oregano, salt, pepper, carrots, and onions. Simmer for 30 minutes. Add potatoes and simmer for 20 minutes. Add peas and simmer for an additional ten minutes. Serve in bowls, garnished with parsley. Serves 8.

Robert H. Fischer of Melville, New York likes to serve this stew to his family and friends.

ROLLED BEEF MATAMBRE

1 round steak, 1 1/2 to 2 lbs.
1 tsp. salt
Freshly ground pepper
3/4 cup thinly-sliced onions
1 cup California dry red wine
3 Tbs. red wine vinegar
1/2 lb. fresh spinach, trimmed,
  washed, and well-drained
3 large carrots, cooked and sliced
  lengthwise
6 large stuffed green olives
1/4 lb. fresh mushrooms, sliced
1 cup very fine bread crumbs
1/4 cup melted butter
1 tsp. paprika
Flour
Oil

NIGHT BEFORE: Trim all fat from steak and remove bone. Pound until flat. Place in glass dish and cover with wine, vinegar, salt, pepper, and onions. Cover and refrigerate overnight.

To assemble, drain steak and place on flat surface (reserving marinade). Place spinach leaves flat on steak: add carrot strips, olives, and sliced mushrooms, evenly arranged. Sprinkle bread crumbs over all. Mix melted butter, paprika, and 2 tablespoons of wine marinade, and drizzle over crumbs. Starting at narrowest end, roll meat tightly and tie securely with string. Coat with flour, and brown in a little oil in a deep, heavy skillet or roasting pan. Turn on oven to 350 degrees. (At higher altitudes, such as Tucson, oven should be set at 375 degrees.) When meat is brown on all sides, drain fat, add remaining marinade including onions. Cover and bake in oven for about two hours or until fork tender.

To serve hot, let stand about ten minutes after removing from oven. Remove strings. Slice meat and pour pan juices over it, and serve immediately. If liquid in pan has cooked down too low, add a little more red wine. To serve cold, place meat roll in glass dish, pour pan juices on, and weight down with a heavy utensil such as an iron skillet. Cover and refrigerate overnight. Slice and serve. Serves 4 to 6.

Myra Marino of Tucson, Arizona, rolls beef into a taste-tempting delight.

BEEF BURGUNDY ELITE

1½ Tbs. shortening
6 medium onions, sliced
3/4 lb. mushrooms, trimmed and
  sliced
3 lbs. boneless beef chuck or round
  steak cut into one inch cubes
1 tsp. salt
1/4 tsp. marjoram
1/4 tsp. thyme
1/8 tsp. pepper
2 Tbs. flour
3/4 cup beef broth
2 cups red California red wine

Melt shortening in large skillet. Cook and stir onions and mushrooms until onions are tender. Remove vegetables. In same skillet, brown meat. Add shortening, mix in flour and broth. Sprinkle seasoning and herbs over meat. Stir into skillet, heat to boiling, stirring constantly. Boil and stir for one minute, stir in wine, cover and simmer 1 1/2 to 2 hours, or until meat is tender (liquid should always cover meat.) If necessary, add more broth and wine, 1 part broth to 2 parts wine. Gently stir in onions and mushrooms. Cook until heated through. Serves 6.

Out in Challis, Idaho, W. D. Wilson is known as the "Cooking Cop." Here's his recipe for stew.

BEEF SUPREME

2 lbs. boneless beef chuck
1 cup California red wine
1/2 cup finely chopped onion
1/2 cup finely chopped carrot
1/2 cup finely chopped celery
1 Tbs. snipped parsley
1 tsp. salt
1/4 tsp. pepper
1/2 tsp. dried thyme
1 bay leaf
1 clove garlic, minced
2 Tbs. oil
1/3 cup beef broth
2 onions, chopped
1 cup sliced carrots
1 cup sliced mushrooms
Salt and pepper
3 Tbs. flour
1/4 cup beef broth

Cut beef into one inch cubes. Place cubes in large plastic bag set in large deep bowl. Add wine, finely chopped onion, carrot, celery, parsley, the 1 tsp. salt, pepper, thyme and bay leaf. Tie bag closed. Cover and refrigerate overnight turning bag several times to redistribute marinade. Drain, reserving marinade. In 4 quart Dutch oven, brown beef, garlic and finely chopped vegetables in hot oil. Add marinade and 1/3 cup broth. Bring to boiling. Reduce heat, cover and simmer 45 minutes. Add onions and sliced carrots. Simmer 10 to 15 minutes. Add mushrooms. Blend flour and remaining broth. Add to Dutch oven and cook until bubbly. Serves 6.

Mrs. Patricia M. Etter in St. Louis, Missouri, suggests you serve her version over rice or noodles.

POT ROAST AU VIN

5 to 6 lb. boned pot roast
2 large potatoes, peeled and halved
4 turnips, peeled and halved
6 carrots, cleaned and halved
2 green chiles, deveined but not
*   seeded*
1 whole large onion
1-10 oz. can beef consomme
6 oz. water
2 Tbs. Worcestershire sauce
Salt and pepper to taste
1 1/2 cups dry California red wine

Place all vegetables in bottom of slow cooker or crock pot. Pour in consomme, water, and Worcestershire sauce. Place roast on top. Sprinkle roast with salt, pepper and 1/2 cup chopped onion. Cook on "high," covered, for 6 hours. Add wine and continue cooking 2 hours longer. Serves 4 to 6.

John O'Connor in Ajo, Arizona, uses an unusual cooking method for his specialty, but the results justify the means.

STIFADO
A Greek Stew

3 1/2 lbs. lean beef stew meat, cut
   into 1 1/2 inch cubes
Salt and fresh ground pepper
1/2 cup butter
2 1/2 lbs. small onions, peeled
1-6 oz. can tomato paste
3/4 cup dry California red wine
2 Tbs. red wine vinegar
1 Tbs. brown sugar
1 clove garlic, minced
1 bay leaf
1 small cinnamon stick
1/2 tsp. whole cloves
1/4 tsp. ground cumin
2 Tbs. currants or raisins

Season meat with salt and pepper. Melt butter in Dutch oven or heavy flame-proof casserole. Add the meat and coat with butter but do not brown. Arrange the onions over the meat. Mix together all the other ingredients and pour over the meat and onions. Cover and simmer gently until meat is very tender, about 3 hours, or bake covered in a 300-degree oven until meat is very tender. If baked, check occasionally to see that sauce is not becoming too dry. Add a little more wine if necessary. Stir gently just before serving. Serves 6.

While stews come in many nationalities, Barbara Karoff of Menlo Park, California, uses a potpourri of interesting ingredients for her favorite.

BURGUNDY BEEF STEW

4 Tbs. olive oil
1 clove garlic, split
2 large onions, sliced
1/3 cup flour
1 1/2 tsp. salt
1/4 tsp. pepper
2 1/2 lbs. stewing beef, cut into 1
   1/2 inch cubes
1/2 tsp. dill weed
1 cup California red wine
1-10 oz. can beef consomme
1-10 oz. package frozen
   artichoke hearts
4 Tbs. butter
18 fresh mushrooms, halved
2-8 oz. packages refrigerator
   biscuits
Melted butter
Parmesan cheese

Heat oil in a heavy kettle. Saute garlic and onions until golden. Remove. Mix flour, salt, and pepper. Dredge meat in mixture and brown well in the same oil, adding more if needed. Return onions to pot. Add dill weed, wine, and consomme. Cover tightly and simmer about 1 1/2 hours or until tender. Cook artichokes one minute less than package directions; add to meat. Melt butter, add mushrooms, and saute 5 minutes. Add to meat. Mix gently, correct seasonings and pour into a 1 1/2 quart casserole (oven proof). Crown with biscuits and bake 15 to 20 minutes in a 400 degree oven. Five minutes before done, brush biscuits with butter and sprinkle with cheese. Bake extra biscuits for dunking. Serves 6.

In Santa Rosa, California, Maryanne Speciale tops her stew with biscuits; a tasty crowning touch.

NATASCHA PEPPER STEAK

1 1/2 lbs. round steak, cut 1/2 inch
* thick*
1/4 cup all purpose flour
1/2 tsp. salt
1/2 tsp. pepper
1/2 tsp. sugar
1/4 cup cooking oil or shortening
1-8 oz. can tomatoes (1 cup)
2 cups beef bouillon
1/2 cup California red wine
1/2 cup chopped onion
1 small clove garlic, minced
1 Tbs. beef-flavor gravy base
1 1/2 tsp. Worcestershire sauce
2 large green peppers, cut in strips
1 1/2 cups celery cut in 1 inch slices

Cut steak in strips, combine flour, salt and pepper; coat meat strips. In large skillet, cook meat in hot oil until browned on all sides. Drain tomatoes, reserving liquid. Add tomato liquid, beef bouillon, sugar, onion, garlic, and gravy base to meat in skillet. Cover and simmer for about 1 1/4 hours, until meat is tender. Uncover; stir in Worcestershire and wine. Add green pepper strips and celery. Cover and simmer 5 to 7 minutes. If necessary, thicken gravy with a mixture of a little flour and cold water. Add drained tomatoes; cook about 5 minutes more, you may wish to add sliced mushrooms. Serve over hot rice. Serves 6.

Mrs. Don Pentz of Venice, Florida, has a special way with pepper steak, and I appreciate it.

BEEF ROLLS IN RED WINE

6 large thin slices of very lean beef
  rump roast
Seasoned salt
1 lb. fresh pork sausage
1 clove garlic, finely minced
1 small onion, finely chopped
1/2 cup parsley, finely minced
6 strips carrot, cut 2" long x 1/4" x
  1/4"
6 strips celery, cut 2" long x 1/4" x
  1/4"
6 Tbs. flour
4 Tbs. vegetable oil
2 cups dry California red wine
1/4 cup tomato sauce
1/2 tsp. salt
1/4 tsp. freshly grated black pepper
1-4 oz. can sliced mushrooms

Sprinkle slices of meat with seasoned salt. Spread a thin layer of pork sausage over each. Sprinkle garlic and onion over each slice, dividing equally. Place 1 strip of carrot and 1 strip of celery on each slice and roll up and tie each end securely with kitchen thread. Roll each beef roll in flour and brown in 12" skillet in the vegetable oil, turning frequently until well browned on all sides. Add wine, tomato sauce, salt, black pepper, and mushrooms. Cover, let simmer slowly for 1 hour over low heat. Remove beef rolls to platter and keep warm. Skim all fat possible from top of sauce. Turn heat to high and boil until sauce is thickened. Moisten each roll with the sauce and serve the balance in a sauce boat. Serves 6.

Rolled-up beef with savory insides has long been a European favorite. This version comes from Mrs. Cleo C. Beeson of Austin, Texas.

SAUTE OF BEEF WITH
PORT AND MUSHROOMS

1½ to 2 lbs. flank or rump steak,
*   cut into 4 even-sized pieces*
3/4 cup California Port
2 cups mushrooms
2 Tbs. butter
1 Tbs. oil
1 Tbs. flour
1 cup beef stock
Salt and pepper
2 cloves of garlic, crushed
1 Tbs. chopped parsley (for garnish)

In a saute pan or skillet heat 1 Tbs. butter and the oil and brown the meat on all sides. Add the Port and flame; simmer until reduced by half. Transfer the meat and liquid to a bowl. Heat the remaining butter in the pan, stir in the flour and cook until straw-colored. Add the stock and bring to a boil, stirring. Put back the meat and liquid. Season, cover and simmer 1 hour. Add the mushrooms and garlic and cook 1/2 hour longer or until the meat is very tender. Taste for seasoning, sprinkle with chopped parsley. Delicious with mashed potatoes. Serves 4.

Port wine has long been a cooking favorite in France. It adds a distinct flavor to a dish, as Mrs. Ruth Hart of Clayton, California, shows us.

FABULOUS FLANK STEAK

2 lbs. flank steak
1/2 cup undiluted beef consomme
1/2 cup California red wine
1/3 cup soy sauce
1 1/2 tsp. seasoned salt
1/4 cup chopped green onions, tops
    and all
1 clove garlic, minced
3 Tbs. lime juice
2 Tbs. brown sugar
2 Tbs. honey

Score the top of the meat into one-inch-wide strips. Marinate in the refrigerator at least eight hours in the marinade made by combining the ingredients listed above. Broil two minutes on each side. Serves 5 to 6.

Flank steak can represent considerable savings when watching the budget. Maile George of Lafayette, California, has an interesting marinade for her flank steak!

STEAK BURGUNDY

1½ lbs. sirloin steak, sliced in
  1-inch strips
3 Tbs. cooking oil
2 cups each sliced onions and
  carrots
1/3 cup California red wine
1-10 1/2 oz. can beef broth
1-4 oz. can sliced mushroom and
  liquid
2 1/2 tsp. seasoned salt
1 Tbs. Worcestershire sauce
2 cups celery, diagonally sliced
2 Tbs. cornstarch
1/4 cup water

Saute steak strips in oil, turning once until brown. Add onions and cook 2 minutes longer. Stir in carrots, wine, broth, mushrooms with liquids and seasonings. Bring to boil. Reduce heat, cover and simmer 10 minutes. Add celery and continue cooking 10 minutes longer. Dissolve cornstarch in water. Stir into meat mixture. Cook, stirring until thick. Serve with rice. Serves 6.

Simple dishes that take a minimum amount of time are always welcomed by busy cooks. Here's a quick main course from Mrs. Blanche Stephenson of Ballwin, Missouri.

SHERRY MEATBALLS

1 ½ lbs. ground chuck
1 ½ cup dried bread crumbs
1 cup minced onion
1 1/2 tsp. cornstarch
Dash of allspice
2 eggs, beaten
1 cup half and half or light cream
1 tsp. salt
1/2 cup shortening
1/3 cup flour
2 cups water
1/2 cup dry California dry Sherry
4 beef bouillon cubes
1 Tbs. brown seasoning sauce
1 tsp. salt

Combine meat, crumbs, onion, cornstarch, allspice, eggs, cream and salt. Mix well and shape into balls. Brown in hot shortening. Transfer meatballs to warm dish. Blend flour with remaining shortening in skillet. Stir in water, Sherry, bouillon cubes and seasonings Cook, stirring until smooth. Arrange meatballs in sauce; cover and simmer about 30 minutes. Serve on rice. Serves 12.

Why do people always seem to associate meatballs with spaghetti? Mrs. Robert F. New of Binghamton, New York, doesn't.

ZESTY BEEF RIBS VIN ROUGE

*3 lbs. beef short ribs, trim off some
  fat
2½ cups California red wine
1/4 tsp. salt
1/8 tsp. pepper
1/2 cup flour
2 Tbs. margarine
2 cans (one lb. each) stewed
  tomatoes
3/4 cup chopped celery, including
  leaves
1/2 tsp. salt
1 tsp. Worcestershire sauce
1/4 tsp. chili powder
1/2 cup seedless raisins
1 Tbs. lemon juice*

Marinate beef short ribs overnight in wine. Combine salt, pepper, and flour. Dredge meat in flour mixture. Melt margarine in electric fry-pan and brown meat on all sides at 360 degrees. Add next 5 ingredients including any leftover wine. Simmer, covered, 2 1/2 hours or until meat is tender. Add raisins and lemon juice. Simmer 10 more minutes. Serve over hot rice or noodles. Serves 4 to 6.

If you would like something different when cooking beef ribs, Mrs. Joan Zimmerman of Santa Rosa, California suggests this tasty tidbit.

BURGUNDY BROILED BEEF PATTIES

1 lb. lean ground beef
1/2 cup soft bread crumbs
1/4 cup California red wine
1 Tbs. Worcestershire sauce
1/4 tsp. marjoram (crushed)
1 tsp. onion salt
1/4 tsp. garlic powder
Dash of pepper

Mix all ingredients well. Cover and refrigerate and let flavors mingle for at least three hours. Shape meat mix into 4 patties. Broil to desired doneness, turning once, catching any juices in foil. Serve on heated platter with juices poured over. Serves 4.

If you are an outdoor-grill person, Mrs. R. Kinyon of Ogden, Utah, thinks you will enjoy this recipe even more.

CANDLELIGHT VEAL

1/2 cup mushrooms
2 Tbs. butter
1 1/2 lbs. veal cubes, trimmed
1 cup red apples, cored and sliced
3 Tbs. sugar
1/3 tsp. poppy seeds
1/3 tsp. parsley
1/3 tsp. all purpose seasoning
3/4 cup California dry white wine
1/2 cup Calvados
Salt and pepper to taste
1/2 cup sour cream
2/3 cup diced almonds

Saute mushrooms in butter for 5 to 7 minutes. In another larger pan, saute veal for about 10 to 12 minutes, stirring frequently. Add mushrooms and all other ingredients except apples, sour cream, and almonds. Cover pan and cook over medium heat for 45 minutes, stirring occasionally. Add apples and continue cooking for another 30 minutes with cover on. Before serving, stir in sour cream thoroughly and sprinkle almonds on top. Serves 2.

This recipe from Sid Goldstein of San Francisco was awarded a certificate of appreciation.

SCALLOPS OF VEAL A LA PORK

8 scallops of veal
1/2 cup grated Parmesan cheese
1-4 oz. bag fried pork skins, finely
  crumbled (reserve 5 skins for
  garnish)
1/4 lb. butter
2 Tbs. onion, finely chopped
1/4 lb. fresh mushrooms, sliced
1 cup California dry white wine
1 cup beef broth
1/2 tsp. salt
1/2 tsp. white pepper
1 Tbs. flour mixed with 1/4 cup
  cold water
1 Tbs. chopped parsley

Pound scallops until very thin. Coat with 1/4 cup cheese and crumbled pork skins. Saute over medium heat in butter until well browned. Transfer to serving dish. In remaining butter, saute onion and mushrooms until soft. Add wine, broth, and seasonings and reduce liquid by boiling for 5 minutes. Add flour and water mixture to pan juices and continue to simmer until thickened. Pour sauce over veal scallops in serving dish. Top with remaining Parmesan, parsley, and coarsely crumbled reserved pork skins. Place in preheated 450 degree oven for 5 to 10 minutes, or until sauce is bubbly and cheese is melted. Serve with buttered fine noodles. Serves 4.

Jerry E. Shannon of Ropesville, Texas serves his scallops this way and made a believer out of me the first time I cooked them.

VEAL WITH SHERRY AND MUSHROOMS

1/4 cup sifted flour
1/4 tsp. nutmeg
1 1/2 tsp. salt
1 1/2 lbs. veal stew meat, cut into
  1/2 inch pieces
4 Tbs. butter or margarine
1 cup chicken broth or bouillon
1/2 cup California Sherry
1/2 lb. fresh mushrooms
1 Tbs. instant minced onion
1 Tbs. finely chopped parsley
Hot cooked rice

Combine flour, nutmeg, salt. Dredge veal in flour mixture and brown in hot butter. Add broth, wine, mushrooms and onion. Cover and simmer until meat is tender, about 1 hour. Just before serving, sprinkle with parsley. Serve over hot rice. Serves 6.

Once again, California Sherry shows its versatility, this time in the capable hands of Jean E. Wederitz of Petaluma, California.

RED WINE AND ROAST VEAL

4 lb. veal boneless rump or sirloin
  roast
2 tsp. salt
1/2 tsp. pepper
4 cloves garlic, crushed
3 Tbs. oil
1/2 cup dry California red wine
1/4 cup water
1 tsp. oregano, crumbled leaf,
  not powdered
1/2 tsp. sugar

Rub surface of roast with salt and pepper. Place roast on rack in open shallow roasting pan. Do not add water or cover. Roast in 325 degree oven for 2 hours. In a small saucepan, gently simmer remaining ingredients except the wine, for 15 minutes. Remove from heat and add the wine. Pour half the sauce mixture over the roast; continue cooking about 1 hour, this time covered. Occasionally brush roast with remaining sauce. Ten minutes before the roast should be done insert a meat thermometer so the tip is in the center of the thickest part of the meat. The thermometer should register 170 degrees. Serves 6 to 8.

There's nothing like roast veal, especially if done well. Meg Cipriano of San Francisco shows how veal and red wine marry to perfection.

VEAL STEW

1/2 cup flour
1/2 tsp. mace
1 tsp. salt
1 tsp. fresh ground pepper
1/2 Tbs. garlic powder
2 lbs. veal shoulder cut into 1 1/2
*   inch pieces*
1/4 cup butter
2 cups chicken stock
3/4 cup onions, chopped
3/4 cup celery, diced
3/4 cup carrots, diced
1 Tbs. capers, rinsed
1 cup California dry white wine

Blend flour, mace, salt, pepper, garlic powder; dredge veal in this mixture. Heat butter in heavy skillet, lightly brown veal on all sides a few pieces at a time, and set aside. Add wine to skillet, bring to boil, scraping pan. Add chicken broth and veal and simmer for one hour. Add onion, celery, carrots and simmer 1/2 hour longer, or until veal is very tender. Add capers and correct seasoning. Serve over boiled white rice and garnish with dill. Serves 6.

Harry Cameron in Sarasota, Florida shares with us his savory veal stew.

PORK

You and I enjoy pork today thanks to Christopher Columbus. He brought eight pigs to the Americas on his second voyage to the New World.

The pig was appreciated some 40,000 years ago. His picture was depicted on the walls of the Altamira caverns in Spain. He was also the emblem of the Roman Twentieth Legion. The Greeks and Romans looked upon the sow as the nourisher of Zeus and, according to Darwin, the Chinese have recognized its value as a food since 5,000 B.C.

The average consumption of pork in the United States is about 56 pounds per year, per person, which by some standards is low. Yet pork is a versatile meat, as we shall see in the following recipes.

ORIENTAL PORK WITH GREENS

About 4 lbs. rolled, boneless pork
loin (cut off all visible fat)
2 Tbs. honey
2 Tbs. peanut oil
1 cup California dry Sherry
3 Tbs. soy sauce
4 cups water
2 lbs. Chinese cabbage, chopped
(may also use green head cabbage
or spinach, or a combination)
1/4 cup toasted sesame seeds

Spread a thin coating of honey on the pork. Using a large kettle, brown pork on all sides in peanut oil. Add Sherry and soy sauce and water. Cover and simmer for about 2 hours or until the meat is very tender. Remove meat from kettle, slice, and keep it warm. Skim fat from broth. Bring broth to boil and add greens. Cover and cook 5 to 10 minutes or until greens are just tender. Serve each slice of pork in a shallow bowl with some greens and broth. Sprinkle one teaspoon toasted seeds on each serving. Serves 6 to 8.

A certificate of appreciation went to A. Kazaks of Sarasota, Florida, for her oriental pork with greens.

PORK CHOPS IN RED WINE

2 Tbs. vegetable oil
6 loin pork chops, cut 1 inch thick
1 clove garlic, finely chopped
2 tsp. fresh chopped oregano
1/2 tsp. fresh chopped thyme
1 tsp. salt
1/2 cup California dry red wine
1 cup tomato sauce
2 green peppers, cut in strips 1/4
  inch wide
1 large onion, cut in strips 1/4 inch
  wide
1-4 ounce can sliced mushrooms
1/4 cup fresh parsley, finely minced

In a large skillet heat vegetable oil until hot. Add pork chops and brown well on both sides. Remove chops. Pour off oil. Add garlic, oregano, thyme and salt. Stir for a few seconds. Add wine and bring to boil, scraping particles from bottom of pan. Add tomato sauce and return chops to pan. Sprinkle peppers, onions, and sliced mushrooms over top. Cover, cook for 1 hour over low heat. Turn chops each 15 minutes and baste with sauce. Remove cover and remove chops to platter and keep warm. Raise heat to high and boil until sauce is thick. Spoon vegetables and sauce over chops. Serves 6.

The chop is one favorite way to serve pork, and this recipe is from Mrs. Cleo C. Beeson of Austin, Texas.

SHERRIED CHOPS WITH RICE

1 Tbs. oil
6 pork chops, cut 1 inch thick
1 large onion, chopped
2 Tbs. margarine
1½ cups raw long grain white rice
1 tsp. salt
1/2 tsp. garlic salt
1/4 tsp. pepper
1-10 oz. can beef boullion
1/2 cup dry California Sherry
Enough water to make 3 cups liquid
*   when combined with the bouillon*
*   and sherry*

Place oil in electric skillet and brown chops. Remove. Melt margarine and add onion, saute until clear. Add rice and brown, turning often. Combine bouillon, Sherry, and water. Pour over rice, leveling rice with fork. Place chops on top. Cover and cook on low, 250 to 275 degrees for 1 1/2 hours. Serves 4 to 6.

The Chinese have been mating pork chops and Sherry in their cooking in recent years. Bernadette Nelson of Phoenix, Arizona, shares her version with us.

STUFFED PORK CHOPS

6 pork chops 1 ½ inch thick with
*   deep pocket in each*
3 sausages removed from casings
3 Tbs. margarine
1/2 cup chopped celery
1 small onion, chopped
3 cups fresh cubed bread
1/2 tsp. salt
1/4 tsp. thyme leaves
1/8 tsp. parsley flakes
Shake sage
Shake chili powder
3/4 cup apple juice
3/4 cup California white wine

Saute crumbled sausage meat, discard fat; wipe frying pan with paper towel. To same pan add margarine and saute celery and onion. Add bread and seasonings; mix well. Lastly add 1/2 cup of apple juice and 1/2 cup of wine. Stuff pork chops with mixture and secure with toothpicks. Place chops in a foil-lined baking pan. Bake uncovered 30 minutes at 450 degrees. Reduce oven to 350 degrees, drain off fat from pan and add additional 1/4 cup apple juice and 1/4 cup of wine. Cover chops with foil and bake 50 to 60 minutes or until tender. If fewer chops are used, decrease ingredients accordingly. Serves 6.

Stuffed pork chops can be a different taste treat, according to Mrs. Maria L. Settimo of Springfield, New Jersey.

BREADED PORK CHOPS IN
WINE AND GARLIC

8 loin or rib pork chops, cut 1/2
   inch thick and trimmed of excess
   fat
1/2 cup unsifted flour
2 eggs
2 tsp. cold water
1 cup toasted bread crumbs
1/2 tsp. salt
1/4 tsp. pepper
1/4 tsp. powdered rosemary
1/4 tsp. powdered sage
1/4 tsp. garlic powder
2/3 cup California dry white wine

Dip chops in unsifted flour to coat, then in egg mixture (eggs and water, beaten.)
Then dip in bread crumb mixture, (bread crumbs, salt, pepper, rosemary, sage
and garlic powder). Let dry on rack at room temperature for 10 minutes. Brown
chops 3 to 4 minutes on each side over moderate heat in a large, heavy skillet
brushed with oil. After chops are browned place on a large flat plate while
preparing wine and garlic sauce. Into juices remaining in fry pan (removed from
heat) add crushed garlic to taste and 1 Tablespoon wine for each chop. Stir until
mixed. In a casserole with a cover, place 4 Tablespoons of the sauce in the
casserole then 4 chops, then repeat. Top with any remaining sauce. Cover and
bake for 50 minutes at 350 degrees. Serves 4.

*And Meg Cipriano of San Francisco enjoys her chops this delightful way; breaded and
cooked in wine and garlic.*

SAUSAGE AND RICE CASSEROLE

1 lb. bulk country sausage
2 large onions, chopped
2 cups uncooked rice
1/4 tsp. crushed sage
1/4 tsp. crushed thyme
1/4 tsp. crushed marjoram
1 1/4 tsp. salt
1-8 oz. can mushroom stems and
*   pieces, drained*
2-10 1/2 oz. cans of beef stock
1 cup water
1 cup California red wine

Fry sausage until crumbly and brown. Pour off excess fat, saving 2 tablespoons. Transfer sausage to casserole dish. Fry onions in reserved sausage fat until translucent. Then add rice to onions and dripping mixture and stir well until rice is well heated. Add herbs, salt, mushrooms, stock, water and wine to rice mix and heat just to simmer. Add heated rice mix to sausage and blend well, spreading evenly in casserole dish. Cover and bake 1 hour at 325 degrees. Serves 6.

With casseroles becoming more and more popular, Mrs. R. Kinyon of North Ogden, Utah, offers her special recipe for you to try.

NATASCHA BURGUNDY
WINE GLAZED HAM

1 fully cooked ham (about 10 to 14
  lbs.)
Whole cloves
1-1 lb. can whole cranberry sauce
1/2 cup brown sugar
1/3 cup bottled steak sauce
1/2 cup California red wine
2 tsp. prepared mustard

Place ham fat side up on rack in shallow pan. Score fat in diamond pattern; stud with whole cloves. Bake at 325 degrees for 2 1/2 to 3 hours. Stir together cranberry sauce, brown sugar, steak sauce, wine, and mustard; simmer, uncovered, 7 minutes. During last 30 minutes baking time for ham, spoon half of cranberry glaze over ham. Serve remaining as sauce. Serves 10.

It used to be that ham was only served at Easter or Christmas. Today ham is so good that it can be served almost anytime, as Mrs. Don Pentz of Venice, Florida does.

L A M B

Mankind has been eating lamb since 9,000 B.C., or so the oldest sheep bones found in Iraq would indicate. Prehistoric man was eating lamb rather than mutton since he slew sheep before they were a year old.

Lamb is held in high esteem by the French as well as the Chinese, Italians and Spanish, while the Austrians pay scant attention to it. The United States is sulky towards lamb—Americans eat only a scant four pounds per person.

LEG OF LAMB WITH BURGUNDY

1 whole leg of lamb, approximately
    7 lbs.
6 cloves garlic, peeled
4 cups California red wine
3 medium onions, peeled and sliced
8 medium potatoes, washed and
    thickly sliced
8 carrots peeled and sliced
1 lb. of fresh mushrooms, cleaned
3 Tbs. sweet basil
2 Tbs. oregano
2 Tbs. parsley flakes
2 tsp. rosemary
2 tsp. thyme
2 tsp. marjoram
Salt and pepper to taste

Place leg of lamb in large roasting pan. Make slits in lamb. Cut garlic cloves in half and place them in the slits. Pour wine over lamb. Sprinkle seasonings over the lamb and in the wine. Surround lamb with onions, potatoes and carrots. Cover and marinate overnight, basting occasionally. Cover and cook 2 1/2 hours at 325 degrees. Uncover, add mushrooms and cook for approximately 1 1/2 hours longer, basting frequently. Let stand 15 minutes before carving. Serve lamb and vegetables with marinade and juice for gravy. Serves 8 to 10 people.

This lamb recipe is a favorite of Joan L. Holland of Ventura, California.

ROAST LAMB "ASADO ARGENTINOS"

1 cup green onions
1 cup parsley or cilantro
1/2 cup green pepper
1/2 cup celery with leaves
1 Jalapeno pepper, remove seeds
2 cloves garlic
2 cups California white wine
2 1/2 cups vegetable oil (or half and
half vegetable oil and olive oil)
1 whole leg of lamb
Salt

Make a marinade of the first eight ingredients and marinade the leg at least nine hours. Lightly rub coarse salt over lamb and place on roasting rack in pan. Put in pre-heated 450 degree oven for 10 minutes, reduce heat to 350 degrees. After 30 minutes, baste meat with marinade. Continue roasting at 15 to 20 minutes per pound, basting with marinade periodically, until done to your taste. The pan juices make an excellent sauce or gravy. Serves 8 to 10.

Cissie Smith of radio station KQEN in Roseburg, Oregon, shares this unusual lamb recipe she obtained from the Argentinos some years ago.

BARBEQUED LEG OF LAMB LAMOUT

1 cup California red table wine
1 cup California white table wine
2 tsp. poultry seasoning
2 tsp. salt
3 cloves garlic, peeled
1 leg of lamb, boned and butterflied

Thoroughly blend wines, poultry seasoning, salt and garlic. Place lamb in glass or porcelain container. Cover with the wine marinade. Leave for at least 12 hours, or as long as 24 hours, turning lamb occasionally. If a tightly covered container is used, this turning can easily be accomplished by turning the container. Barbeque meat over coals, skin side up for 1/2 hour, basting frequently with marinade. Turn meat, continuing cooking and basting for an additional 30 minutes. Total cooking time is 1 hour. Serves 6 to 8.

Out in Bensalem, Pennsylvania, Ruth Roberts uses a white California wine with a red meat, and it does make a special dish.

LAMB STEW LAWSON

*3 lb. boneless lamb shoulder,
    trimmed of fat and cut in one
    inch cubes
2 Tbs. safflower oil
12 oz. package of fresh baby carrots
1 bunch of scallions, chopped
3 stalks of celery sliced into small
    pieces
1½ cups California white wine
1½ cups consomme
2 oz. lemon juice
2 cloves garlic, crushed
1 bay leaf
2 tsp. rosemary
Pinch of tarragon
1½ tsp. oregano
1 tsp. marjoram
1/2 tsp. paprika
2 tsp. lemon pepper
2 tsp. seasoned salt
1 can of whole white potatoes*

Brown lamb in electric frying pan, use small amount of safflower or sunflower oil. When brown, drain excess oil and place lamb in a Dutch oven. Saute carrots, scallions, and celery briefly in the same oil; drain and add to Dutch oven. Add wine, consomme, and lemon juice to Dutch oven. Add all seasonings. Cook over very low heat. After one hour, add potatoes. Simmer over very low heat for an additional hour and a half. Serves 6.

Here's a lamb stew that is a meal in itself, according to Harry O. Lawson of the University of Denver College of Law.

LAMB, HUNTER'S STYLE

2½ lbs. lamb shoulder, cut into
  one inch pieces
2 cups onions, chopped
1/2 cup olive oil
2/3 cup dry California red wine
1/4 cup California brandy
Salt
1/2 tsp. grated nutmeg
1/2 tsp. thyme
1/4 tsp. ground cloves
12 peppercorns, lightly crushed
2 cloves garlic, minced
2 bay leaves
1/2 cup chicken stock
2 Tbs. butter
2 Tbs. olive oil
Peel of one orange, cut in a spiral
6 juniper berries

Combine lamb, onions, 1/2 cup olive oil, wine, brandy, salt, nutmeg, thyme, cloves, peppercorns, juniper berries, garlic and bay leaves in a large bowl. Refrigerate covered for 2 to 3 days. Toss meat every 10 to 12 hours. Add chicken stock and orange peel to the marinade and allow to stand at room temperature for 1 hour. Drain the lamb and pat dry with paper towels. In a heavy skillet melt butter and add 2 tablespoons olive oil. Saute the meat over medium heat until brown on all sides. In a Dutch oven heat marinade to boiling. Reduce heat and simmer until marinade is reduced to 1 1/4 cups. Add the lamb. Cover and bake at 250 degrees for a 1 1/2 to 2 hours. Transfer to a serving dish and garnish with boiled new potatoes. If the sauce seems too thin, remove the lamb when it is done, reduce the sauce over high heat to desired consistency and combine it again with the meat before serving. Serves 4 to 6.

Lamb has been a hunter's meat for hundreds of years. Barbara Karoff of Menlo Park, California, uses a variety of spices for her lamb dish, one that reminds you of the ancient dishes cooked over an open fire.

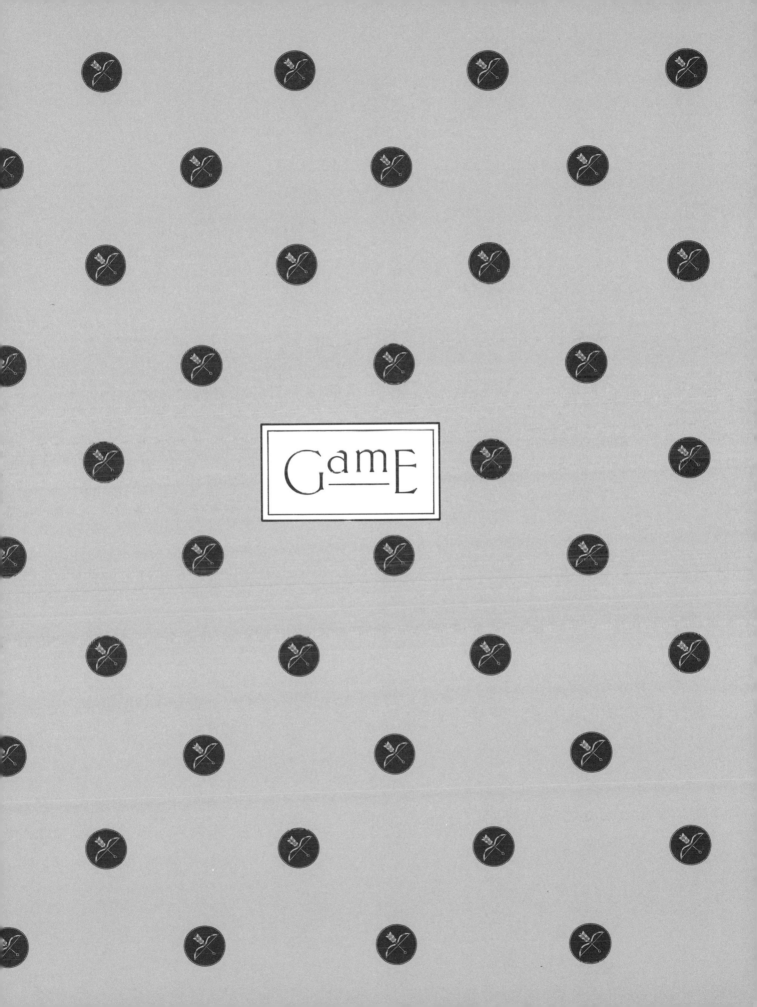

GamE

GAME

There are two reasons why game is not on more menus. First, it is not as plentiful as it once was, and secondly, the taste of game varies from year to year depending upon what they can find to eat.

Years ago, friends in Wisconsin would hunt deer every year. One year the deer would taste great, while the next the meat was bitter and needed days in a marinade. The year the deer tasted good was the year the deer found plenty to eat while the year in which the deer meat was bitter was a year they probably ate roots and tree bark just to survive.

And this is why the popularity of game breeders has increased over the past 20 years. Their game always tastes good, since it is bred and raised under controlled conditions. But game, whether hunted or bought from a purveyor, remains an uncommon entree.

VENISON KABOBS

2 cups California red wine
1 tsp. salt
1 cup tomato puree
12 whole black peppercorns
2 bay leaves
6 cloves garlic, minced
2 whole onions, sliced
3 lbs. cubed venison
18 small whole onions
18 medium sized mushrooms
18 cherry tomatoes
9 slices of bacon
9 skewers

Mix wine, salt, tomato puree, peppercorns, bay leaves, minced garlic, sliced onions, and venison. Cover and let marinate 24 hours. Blanch the small onions, mushrooms and tomatoes. Arrange the venison, onions, and mushrooms on the skewers while placing one-third piece of bacon on each side of venison. Cook over an open fire. Serves 4.

Elaine J. Geise of the Culinary Institute of America in Hyde Park, New York enjoys cooking venison using this kabob recipe.

VENISON ROAST SUPREME

*1 lb. (approximately) fresh pork or
beef suet, cut in small pieces
1-8 to 10 lb. venison roast, at room
   temperature
3 cups of California red wine
1 cup of salad oil
2 cloves of garlic
2 tsp. salt
2 tsp. black pepper
1 Tbs. Worcestershire sauce
2 Tbs. catsup
1 tsp. dry mustard
1/2 tsp. cloves
1/2 tsp. nutmeg
2 sliced apples
2 sliced onions
3 sliced potatoes*

Work pieces of pork into creases of venison to the bone. Mix next 10 ingredients. Place roast in large pan, pour over sauce, dipping it back over meat. Marinate overnight in refrigerator. Brown roast on all sides in hot skillet; place in large roaster with marinade and about 2 cups of hot water. Place apples, onions and potatoes over meat. Cover. Bake at 300 degrees until tender, basting often. A little flour may be used on roast before browning if desired. Serves 10.

Here is an original recipe from Annie Laurie Spencer of El Dorado, Arkansas, whose family lives on a Delta plantation.

GAME IN WINE SAUCE

6 halved small game birds (pigeons,
*   cornish hens or small ducks) or 3*
*   quartered larger ducks*
2 finely minced onions
2 heaping Tbs. flour
1/3 tsp. thyme or large sprig of fresh
sprig of basil
2 cloves
1 to 2 bay leaves, depending on size
A dash of allspice
Salt
3/4 cup California red wine
1/2 lb. mushrooms, cleaned and
*   sliced, or whole if small*

Brown birds in oil in a heavy pan, preferrably a cast iron Dutch oven. Remove the birds and saute the onions in the leftover oil until transparent. Add the birds and the flour and stir well. Cover with hot water and add the spices (spices may be placed in spice bag for easy removal.) Salt to taste and cook covered until the game is fork tender. Add the wine and mushrooms and simmer until the mushrooms are cooked. Serves 4.

Here's a versatile recipe from Jacqueline Pelton in Vacaville, California, in which the flavor of the various birds is enhanced by the sauce.

VENISON PAPRIKA

3 lbs. venison steak
1/2 cup flour
Salt and pepper
Few grains cayenne pepper
1/3 cup butter
1 large onion, finely chopped
4 cloves garlic, finely chopped
1 tsp marjoram
1⅛ cup California dry Sherry
2 Tbs. paprika
1 can (16 oz.) whole tomatoes,
*   chopped, but not drained*
1 cup sour cream

Cut steaks into one inch cubes. In a brown paper bag, place the flour, salt, pepper and cayenne pepper. Shake up cubes of steak until dusted. In a large skillet melt the butter. When hot, add cubes of steak and lightly brown them. Remove steak and to the pan add the chopped onion, garlic, 1 teaspoon marjoram, tomatoes (juice and all,) Sherry, and paprika. Cook slowly with lid on skillet for 15 minutes. Add the browned steak, replace lid on skillet and cook slowly until venison is tender (45 minutes to 1 hour). Stir in 1 cup commercial sour cream and serve. Serves 6.

Melba Beken of Rosharon, Texas, makes venison extra special with this recipe.

VENISON BOURGUIGNON

3 lbs. trimmed venison, cut in 1 ½
   inch cubes
2 cups California Petite Syrah
1 cup dry California Sherry
1/2 cup olive oil
2 tsp. soy sauce
2 cloves garlic
1/2 tsp. thyme
2 bay leaves
dash of Tabasco
3 medium onions, thinly sliced
1 cup flour
salt and pepper to taste
Accent to taste
butter
1 cup beef stock
2 large carrots, sliced
2 onions, sliced
1/2 lb. fresh mushrooms, sliced

Place venison in a glass or stainless steel bowl. Combine red wine, Sherry, oil, soy sauce, garlic, thyme, bay leaves, Tabasco and 1 onion. Pour over meat and marinate for 4 hours, shaking and turning meat a few times. If desired, tenderize the venison and keep in marinade for 2 more hours. Drain and dry meat, reserving marinade. Season flour with salt, pepper and Accent, and put in a plastic sack. Dredge a few cubes of venison at a time. Brown meat in a heavy skillet without crowding. Remove and keep warm while browning rest of meat. Add 1 cup of strained marinade to heavy skillet and scrape all brown bits which will form base of stew. Return all meat to skillet, and add rest of marinade and beef stock. If there is not enough liquid to cover meat, add wine or Sherry. After simmering for 1 hour, add carrots, 2 onions, and mushrooms, sauteed in butter. Simmer for 2 1/2 hours or until meat is tender. Serves 6.

In Dallas, Texas, Victor Wdowiak serves his friends choice venison with two California wines in the dish, and more as an accompaniment.

NORMANDY STYLE RABBIT

1-3 1/2 to 4 lb. rabbit, cut up,
*   reserving the liver and kidneys*
4 Tbs. butter
1 large onion, sliced into rings
Salt and pepper to taste
1 fifth California Champagne
1 bouquet of herbs (thyme, bay leaf,
*   parsley, marjoram, tied in a*
*   cheesecloth bag)*
1/2 cup California brandy

In a dutch oven or large frying pan, saute rabbit pieces in butter, do not brown. Add sliced onion rings to fried rabbit. Saute onion until golden, add salt and pepper to taste, Champagne, bring to a boil and add herbs, liver and kidneys. Reduce heat and simmer for 1 1/2 hours, half covered to allow concentration of juices. Add brandy and flambe. Cover completely, cook 5 minutes longer, and serve hot. Serves 4 to 6.

Rabbit is appearing in more and more stores these days and Denise M. Sutter in San Jose, California, likes to cook it with California Champagne and brandy.

Vegetables

VEGETABLES

I first tasted vegetables that had been cooked in wine more than 20 years ago. Sliced red onions had been slowly simmered in equal parts of California Maderia and beef stock until they had cooked down to a glaze. They were served as a side dish to accompany a charcoal-broiled steak. They were exceptional, and I still serve them today.

BRAISED CARROTS AND FENNEL

1 Tbs. each butter and margarine
4 carrots, cut in strips about 2
*   inches long*
1 fennel bulb, cut in strips, same
*   thickness as carrots*
1/2 cup California dry white wine
1 package instant chicken broth

Place butter and margarine in saucepan. Add carrots and fennel, stirring to make sure pieces are coated. Cook about 3 to 4 minutes on medium heat. Add wine and 1/4 cup water to which the chicken broth packet has been mixed. Cover saucepan and cook over low heat for 20 to 30 minutes. Vegetables should be just crisp tender. Remove vegetables and liquid may be boiled for a few minutes to reduce to 1/2 cup. Pour over vegetables. Serves 4.

Sometimes two vegetables cooked together play off each other's tastes, as Mrs. M. Louise DiManno of Hamilton Square, New Jersey, shows us.

ZUCCHINI IN WHITE WINE SAUCE

2 cups zucchini, cut in circles
1/2 cup yellow onion
2 Tbs. butter or margarine
1 1/2 to 2 Tbs. flour
1 cup half and half
1/4 cup California white wine
2 Tbs. chopped parsley
1/4 tsp. Worcestershire sauce
1/2 tsp. celery salt

Steam zucchini and onions until lightly tender. Melt butter over a low heat. Add flour, stirring constantly until well blended and there's no raw flour taste. Stir in half and half slowly. Stir until smooth and bubbly. Add 1 1/2 tsp. parsley, Worcestershire, celery salt and stir. Then slowly stir in wine. Allow sauce to lightly bubble, stirring constantly. Remove from heat. Put zucchini in small casserole dish and spoon sauce over top. Sprinkle with remaining parsley. Heat until bubbly in a 350 degree oven. Serves 4.

Another zucchini lover is Debbie Dobosz of San Francisco, who makes hers this way.

SCALLOP SUMMER SQUASH

4 large summer squash
1 1/2 cups California dry Sherry
3 eggs
1 cup Monterey cheese, shredded
1 medium onion, chopped fine
4 cloves garlic, chopped fine
2 stalks celery, chopped fine
1 cup seasoned bread crumbs
1 sprig parsley

Scoop out center of squash, and par-boil the shells in water and one cup Sherry to cover, until tender. Drain and set aside. In medium saucepan par-boil the inside of squash until tender and drain, then mash. In a bowl combine mashed squash with three beaten eggs, the cheese, onion, garlic, celery, and bread crumbs. Add 1/2 cup Sherry. Salt to taste. Spoon into well-drained shells, sprinkle with parsley. Bake in low oven 250 degrees for 30 minutes. Put a little oil in pan before arranging shells to prevent sticking. Serves 4.

Summer squash is one of the midyear delights that can be served in several interesting ways. Flora Murray of Rohnert Park, California, created this recipe.

PENNSYLVANIA DUTCH
RED BEETS AND EGGS

6 hard-cooked eggs
1 #2 can whole beets
1/2 cup California white wine
1/2 cup vinegar
1 cup beet juice from can
1 Tbs. pickling spice

Place eggs and beets in a jar, 2 quarts or larger. Put wine, vinegar, beet juice, pickling spice in pan and bring to simmer. Pour over the eggs and beets in jar. Let stand in refrigerator for a day until the eggs take on the red, beet color. Eggs may be added to replace those used. Serves 3.

Here is an original recipe from the Pennsylvania Dutch country, as given to us by Mrs. Louise Voorhees of West Trenton, New Jersey.

WINE-LOVER'S RICE

2 Tbs. butter or margarine
1/2 cup white long grain rice
1/2 cup vermicelli, broken into 1/4
  inch pieces
1/4 tsp. each Italian herb
  seasoning, salt, garlic salt,
  oregano
Dash of lemon pepper
2 cups hot chicken broth
1/2 cup California dry Vermouth

Melt the butter or margarine in a large pan. Saute the rice and vermicelli until browned. As it is cooking, season with the spices, stirring often so the rice and vermicelli does not stick. When browned, stir in the hot chicken broth and Vermouth. When it comes to a boil, turn heat to low, cover and simmer for 30 minutes. Serves 4.

Rice, though technically a grain, is often served as a vegetable course. Sidney C. Kaffury in San Rafael, California, uses California Vermouth to add a special flavor to his rice dish.

DILLY CUCUMBERS

1 cucumber
1 tsp. salt
1/2 cup sour cream
4 tsp. California dry Sherry
2 Tbs. snipped chives
1/2 tsp. dried dill weed
Bottled hot sauce
Pepper

Thinly slice cucumber; sprinkle with salt; let stand 30 minutes. Drain. Combine sour cream, Sherry, chives, dill weed, and 1 to 2 drops hot sauce; pour over cucumber. Sprinkle with pepper; chill 30 minutes. Serve. Serves 4.

Since cucumbers are available almost throughout the year, this recipe should be a part of your menu planning, thanks to Allen Mills of Albany, California.

CLASSIC MUSHROOMS

2 lbs. fresh mushrooms
1/4 cup butter
1 tsp. olive oil
1/8 cup onions, minced
1/2 tsp. parsley
1/4 tsp. oregano
1/2 tsp. salt
1/4 tsp. pepper
1/2 tsp. sweet basil
1/2 tsp. garlic salt
3/4 cup California white wine
10 oz. sour cream
1/4 cup plus Parmesan cheese,
   grated

Rinse and slice mushrooms. Melt butter, add olive oil and onions. Saute onions on low heat until soft. Add mushrooms and cook for five minutes. Add seasonings and wine and cook on medium heat for about 10 minutes, or until about one-half of the wine has evaporated. Add sour cream and cheese and cook for an additional 10 minutes. Pour into serving dish and sprinkle with additional cheese. Garnish with parsley. Serves 6.

Nancy Griego, assistant to the Editor of the Albuquerque Tribune in Albuquerque, New Mexico, likes mushrooms and shares this recipe with us.

JEANS BEANS

4 slices bacon
1 bunch green onions, chopped
1/2 cup green bell pepper, chopped
2-15 oz. cans red kidney beans
1/4 cup California Port
2 cups cubed lean ham

Fry bacon semi-crisp and remove from pan. In bacon drippings, saute green onions and green pepper until soft but not brown. Add kidney beans (do not drain) and wine. Stir gently and simmer for 10 minutes uncovered. Remove from heat and add ham. Add more wine if desired. Pour entire mixture into 2-quart casserole, put bacon strips on top, cover and bake in 325 degree oven for 30 minutes. Serve with corn bread. Serves 6.

There are many recipes using beans, for they have become one of the staples of the American diet. The way Mrs. Mary Jo Phillips of Dallas, Texas, simmers hers in California Port makes an interesting difference.

SAUTEED SHERRY ZUCCHINI

4 small zucchini
1 tsp. salt
1/4 tsp. dill weed
1/4 tsp. celery seed
1 Tbs. olive oil
1 clove garlic, halved
1/4 cup California dry Sherry

Clean zucchini with vegetable brush, but do not peel. Slice zucchini into 1/2 inch slices. Sprinkle salt, dill weed and celery seed on zucchini; let stand 10 minutes. In heavy skillet, saute garlic until browned; discard. Add zucchini to hot oil in skillet. Cover and saute 3 minutes, shaking skillet frequently. Discard excess liquid. Add Sherry. Reduce heat, cover and simmer 5 minutes. Serves 4.

Zucchini is one of those vegetables that lends itself to many variations on the theme. This one comes from Wendell Anderson of Eugene, Oregon.

Desserts

DESSERTS

Wine has long played a major role in desserts. The simplest dessert has always been fruit and wine, and no one knows this better than the Californians, who have an abundance of both available.

Ices have become sudden favorites and when laced with cream Sherry, California Champagne or a late harvest California wine, they become an important part of any menu.

KIWI FLAN

6 kiwi fruit
1/4 cup California white wine
1/3 cup granulated sugar

1 cup milk
1/3 cup granulated sugar
3 eggs
1 Tbs. vanilla extract
1/8 tsp. salt
2/3 cup sifted all-purpose flour
1 paper lace doily
Shaker of powdered sugar

Preheat oven to 350 degrees. Lightly butter a 9 inch pie plate about 1 1/2 inches deep. Pare and slice kiwi fruit and let stand at least one hour in wine and sugar mixture. Place milk, sugar, eggs, vanilla, salt and flour in blender jar in order listed. Cover and blend at top speed for one minute. Add wine/sugar drained from kiwi fruit and mix in thoroughly.

Pour a 1/4 inch layer of batter in a baking dish or pie plate. Set over moderate heat on range for a minute or two until a film of batter has set in bottom of the dish. Remove from heat and spread kiwi fruit over the batter, reserving some slices for garnish. Pour in the rest of the batter and smooth the surface with the back of a spoon. Place in middle position of preheated oven and bake for one hour. Flan is done when it has puffed and browned and a knife inserted in center comes out clean. Allow to cool, and cover with a paper doily. Sprinkle powdered sugar thickly over doily, then carefully remove doily so lacy pattern will appear on flan. Decorate cake plate with remaining sections of kiwi fruit. Serves 6.

Barbara Morgan of Walnut Creek, California won a certificate of appreciation by the judges for her dessert with America's new fruit favorite, kiwi.

ROYAL WINE PUFFS

Chablis creme:
1/3 cup sugar
3 Tbs. cornstarch
3 egg yolks, slightly beaten
1 cup milk
1/2 cup California Chenin Blanc

Wine puffs:
1/2 tsp. vanilla
1 Tbs. butter
1 cup California Chenin Blanc
1/2 cup butter
1 cup sifted flour
4 eggs
8 strawberries or raspberries
Confectioner's sugar

CHABLIS CREME:
   In a small saucepan, combine sugar and cornstarch. Combine the yolks, milk, and wine and slowly add to the dry ingredients. Stir to boil over medium heat and stir 1 minute. Add vanilla and butter. Remove from burner. Refrigerate.
WINE PUFFS:
   Bring 1 cup wine and butter to a roaring boil in medium sauce pan. Add flour all at once and stir until it forms a ball. Remove from burner and add eggs, one at a time, beating vigorously after each. Using a teaspoon or pastry bag, form dough into 2-inch puffs on ungreased cookie sheets. Depending upon size, you should have a total of around 24 puffs. Bake in pre-heated 400 degree oven for 20 to 30 minutes or until golden brown. Remove from oven and let cool.
   Chop strawberries into tiny bits. Using a small, sharp knife cut and remove top of each puff. Remove inner dough with the knife tip or sharp spoon and discard. Fill each puff with the Chablis creme and insert fruit bit. Replace top of puff. Repeat with the rest of the wine puffs and chablis creme. When completed, sprinkle tops generously with the confectioner's sugar.

Over in Frazier, Pennsylvania, Ms. Jacqueline McComas likes to serve these royal wine puffs to her guests. The judges liked what they tasted and awarded her a certificate of appreciation.

DOSS DELIGHT

8 eggs
1 1/2 cups sugar
Rind of 1 lemon grated
2 Tbs. Kirsch or 1/4 tsp. almond
  flavoring and 1 Tbs. Rum
1 1/2 cups fine breadcrumbs
1 1/2 cups ground walnuts
1 cup California white wine or
  Sherry
3/4 cup sugar
1 stick of cinnamon
8 cloves

Separate eggs. Beat yolks and sugar until thick and lemony. Beat in lemon rind and Kirsch. Fold in nuts and crumbs. Beat egg whites until they stand in soft curls. Fold whites into yolk mixture gently. Butter a 10 inch spring-form pan. Dust lightly with crumbs, then shake out extra crumbs from pan. Fill pan with cake mixture and bake in a low oven preheated to 275 degrees F about 1 1/2 hours. While cake is baking, make a syrup with the wine, sugar, cinnamon and cloves. Heat all in a small saucepan to the boiling point, then simmer for 5 minutes on low heat. Set aside, after removing spices, until cake is baked. Spoon slowly over cake while both syrup and cake are still warm. Serve topped with whipped cream or fresh fruit, berries or melon balls if desired. The cake is good, with or without topping. Serves 6.

Here is a cake from San Francisco's Margot Patterson Doss. The judges agreed it was something special, and awarded her a certificate of appreciation.

PEACHES AND KIWI

6 fresh peaches, peeled and sliced
4 Kiwi, peeled and sliced into thin
rounds
Juice of 4 oranges
3 ounces sweet California white
wine such as Late Harvest
Reisling or Muscat Canelli
Fresh mint leaves

Put the sliced peaches and kiwi into a bowl. Add the orange juice and wine. Toss gently, being careful not to break the fruit. When blended, garnish with mint leaves. Refrigerate for several hours before serving. Serves 6.

In Healdsburg, California, Barbara Bowman claims this is a true California dessert, since all the ingredients grow so well in California.

CABERNET SHERBET

2 Tbs. gelatin
2 cups California Cabernet
  Sauvignon
1 cup sugar
1 cup water
2 Tbs. lemon juice
2 egg whites

Soften gelatin in 1/4 cup Cabernet. Boil the sugar and water for 10 minutes. Add gelatin, the remaining 1 3/4 cups of wine, and lemon juice to the syrup, and stir. Put in refrigerator tray and freeze to a mushy consistency. Place in chilled bowl and beat. Fold in stiffly beaten egg whites and finish freezing. Yield: 1 1/2 quarts.

John Angle of Dakota, Illinois, uses California Cabernet Sauvignon for this special meal-ender.

PEACHES CALIFORNIA

3 lbs. fresh California peaches
1/2 lb. fresh bing cherries
1/2 cup sugar
1 tsp. cornstarch
1/2 tsp. salt
1 cup California Chenin Blanc
2 Tbs. lemon juice
2 Tbs. butter

Peel peaches, holding over dish to catch juices. Slice. Wash and slice cherries in half, removing pits. Set aside. In a small saucepan, combine sugar, cornstarch and salt. Add wine and lemon juice and stir until well blended. Add butter and cook over medium heat, stirring until it boils, thickens and then becomes clear. Remove from heat and pour immediately over fruit. Stir once, cover and refrigerate at least two hours. (Overnight is even better.) Serve as a light dessert or as a first course for brunch. Serves 6 to 8.

Fresh fruit and California Chenin Blanc are a delicious combination, and the prime ingredients of Anaheim's Ruth L. Falk's dessert.

GLAZED STRAWBERRIES SUPREME

*Fresh whole strawberries, washed
and cored (enough to fill 4 tall
sherbet glasses)
1 pint frozen raspberries in syrup
1/4 cup of California cream Sherry
Whipped cream topping*

Place whole strawberries in tall dessert glasses. In a blender or processor, blend raspberries with wine. Pour mixture over strawberries to produce a glazed effect on strawberries. Top with a spoon of whipped cream. Serves 4.

Here's an easy dessert that can be made almost while the salad course is being served, says Mrs. Maria L. Settiro of Springfield, New Jersey.

CABERNET DRIED FRUIT

*1 lb. mixed dried fruit (apricots,
   prunes, raisins, pears, peaches,
   etc.)
1/2 to 3/4 cup sugar
California Cabernet Sauvignon to
   cover
1-2 inch stick cinnamon
Thin strips of lemon peel
Whipped cream*

Rinse the fruit in cold water. Cover with the wine and soak for 12 hours. Add the sugar, spice and lemon peel. Simmer over low heat until the fruit is very soft. Lift out fruit, spice and lemon peel with a slotted spoon and discard spice and lemon peel. Cook the syrup down to a thick consistency. Cool and pour over the fruit. Chill thoroughly and serve topped with whipped cream. Serves 6.

Dried fruits can play an important part in the wine and fruit dessert picture, as Janet Wallach of Bryn Mawr, Pennsylvania, shows us.

FRESH FRUIT SUPREME

3 cups California red wine
3/4 cup granulated sugar
2 Tbs. ground cinnamon
2 tsp. ground nutmeg
1/2 pint fresh strawberries
3 peaches, sliced
2 oranges, peeled and sliced
2 apples, cored and sliced
2 pears, cored and sliced
1 small bunch seedless green grapes
Juice from one whole lemon

In a saucepan, combine wine, sugar and spices. Bring to a boil, reduce to a simmer. Add fresh fruit (except for grapes) and juice from lemon. Simmer 10 minutes. Add grapes. Cover and cool in refrigerator. Serve in wine glass with freshly whipped cream. Serves 6.

Wine, fruit and spices add up to an excellent dessert from Joan L. Holland of Ventura, California.

BELOVED ZINFANDEL CAKE

2 1/4 cups sifted cake flour
2 1/4 tsp. baking powder
1/2 tsp. cinnamon
1/2 tsp. ground clove
1/2 tsp. salt
1/4 cup butter
1/4 cup vegetable shortening
1 cup sugar
3 Tbs. grated orange rind
1/2 cup ground walnuts
2/3 cup California Zinfandel
1/3 cup buttermilk
1 Tbs. orange liquor
4 egg whites
1/4 cup sugar

Grease and flour two 9 inch cake pans. Pre-heat oven to 375 degrees. Mix together the first five ingredients. In a large bowl, cream the butter and shortening. Add 1 cup sugar and grated orange rind. Cream until fluffy. Combine Zinfandel, buttermilk and the orange liquor. Now add the flour mixture, walnuts, and the Zinfandel mixture to the creamed butter mixture and stir until smooth. Whip the egg whites until foamy. Gradually beat in, by the spoonful, the sugar. Continue beating the egg whites until stiff then fold into the cake batter lightly. Place the batter in the cake pans and bake for 25 to 30 minutes. Cool and frost with Orange Cream Frosting (see recipe on following page).

Zinfandel is one of those California wines that wine lovers like to discover over and over again. Here is a whole new way to discover it, from Robert Dixon of Santa Cruz, California.

ORANGE CREAM FROSTING

6 Tbs. butter
2 Tbs. sour cream
1 box, 1 lb. powdered sugar
1 Tbs. thawed orange-pineapple
   juice concentrate
1 tsp. orange liquor

Beat butter and sour cream until fluffy. Beat in orange pineapple juice concentrate, orange liquor, and the powdered sugar. Serves 10.

INDEX

CONTRIBUTORS

Adams, Mary J.
Saratoga, CA 71
Alvar, James E.
Kingman, AZ 93
Anderson, Betty B.
Avon, CT 69
Anderson, Wendell
Eugene, OR 157
Angle, John
Dakota, IL 165
Beeson, Cleo C.
Austin, TX 109, 124
Beken, Melba
Rosharon, TX 144
Bolton, John
Snowbird, UT 95
Bordessa, Vicki
Santa Rosa, CA 96
Bove, Gloria T.
Bethlehem, PA 88
Bowman, Barbara
Healdsburg, CA 164
Brown, Mrs. J.B.
Casa Grande, AZ 52
Cameron, Harry
Sarasota, FL 120
Cipriano, Meg
San Francisco, CA 119, 127
Conley, Mrs. R.T.
Sarasota, FL 79
Coppenbarger, Norma Jean
Sacramento, CA 76
Creager, Janet
Spokane, WA 63
Deeds, Mrs. John W.
Sarasota, FL 77
De Santis, Shirley
Bethlehem, PA 75
Di Manno, Louise
Hamilton Square, NJ 149
Dixon, Robert
Santa Cruz, CA 170, 171
Dobosz, Debbie
San Francisco, CA 150
Doss, Margot Patterson
San Francisco, CA 163
Duncan, Robert E.
Rhineback NY 34
Ericson, Barbara
Loomis, CA 35
Etter, Patricia
St. Louis, MO 104
Falk, Ruth
Anaheim, CA 166
Fischer, Robert
Melville, NY 101
Fogelsong, Libia
San Bruno, CA 89
Fowler, Betty
Los Altos, CA 47
Frazier, Betty
Nokomis, FL 51, 64
Gasparro, Lois
Charlottesville, VA 83

Grise, Elaine
Hyde Park, NY 141
George, Maile
Lafayette, CA 111
Gibbon, Mr. & Mrs. Harlow
Spokane, WA 49
Goldstein, Sid
San Francisco, CA 116
Griego, Nancy
Albuquerque, NM 155
Gross, Irene
Amston, CT 42
Hampton, Mel
Dallas, TX 73
Harmatiuk, Karen
Santa Clara, CA 99-100
Hart, Ruth
Clayton, CA 110
Hathaway, Maruja
Austin, TX 91
Hicks, Julie
Fresno, CA 74
Hill, Janet
Rodeo, CA 55
Holland, Joan L.
Ventura, CA 133, 169
Hornick, Mildred
Dumont, NJ 56
Jacome, Barbara
Rocky Hill, CT 38
Kaffury, Sidney C.
San Rafael, CA 153
Karoff, Barbara
Menlo Park, CA 45, 58, 78, 106, 137
Kazaks, Alexandra
Sarasota, FL 46, 123
Kinyon, Mrs. R.
Ogden, UT 65, 115, 128
Lawson, Harry O.
Denver, CO 136
Malork, Lilli
Vallejo, CA 33
Marino, Myra
Tucson, AZ 37, 102
May, Louise
New York, NY 80
McComas, Jacqueline
Frazier, PA 162
McFerrin, Lee
Denver, CO 60
Meyers, Eliska B.
San Francisco, CA 70, 87
Mills, Allen
Albany, CA 154
Morgan, Barbara
Walnut Creek, CA 57, 161
Mower, Hazel
Garden Grove, CA 66
Murray, Flora
Rohnert Park, CA 151
Nelson, Bernadette
Phoenix, AZ 125

New, Mrs. Robert
Binghamton, NY 113
Nicolaus, Marian
Phoenix, AZ 48, 86
Neilson, Nan
Eureka, CA 59
O'Connor, John
Ajo, AZ 105
Overeem, Sharnette
Wichita, KS 53
Pelton, Jacqueline
Vacaville, CA 143
Pentz, Mrs. Don
Venice, FL 108, 129
Phillips, Mary Jo
Dallas, TX 156
Powell, Pearl
Chicago, IL 36
Riley, Lynn
Walnut Creek, CA 92
Roberts, Ruth
Bensalem, PA 135
Ross, Mrs. Robert
Sonora, CA 39
Settimo, Maria L.
Springfield, NJ 90, 126, 167
Seyfert, Lynn
Idaho Falls, ID 40
Shannon, Jerry B.
Ropesville, TX 72, 117
Slotkin, Reba
Sarasota, FL 84
Smith, Cissie
Roseburg, OR 134
Speciale, Maryanne
Santa Rosa, CA 107
Spencer, Annie Laurie
El Dorado, AR 142
Stephenson, Blanche
Ballwin, MO 112
Sutter, Denise M.
San Jose, CA 54, 146
Valerie, Nessie
Pico River, CA 41
Voorhees, Louise
West Trenton, NJ 152
Wallach, Janet
Bryn Mawr, PA 168
Watt, Lois B.
Stanford, CA 94
Wdowiak, Victor
Dallas, TX 145
Wederitz, Jean E.
Petaluma, CA 118
Williams, Mrs. Ben
Davis, CA 48
Wilson, W.D.
Challis, ID 103
Witkowski, Des.
Phoenix, AZ 50
Zimmerman, Joan
Santa Rosa, CA 114

The Wine Appreciation Guild Books
"The Classic Series on Cooking With Wine"

This series of wine cookbooks is the largest collection of cooking with wine recipes available in the world. There is no duplication of features or recipes in the Wine Advisory Board Cookbooks. Specific wine types are recommended as table beverages for all main dishes. The present series represents over 4,000 different recipes of all types using wine. The magnitude of this collection of wine recipes is remarkable: from wine cocktails, hors d'oeuvres, salads, soups, wild game, fish, eggs, many different main dishes to desserts and jellies. Who could possibly develop and test such a large number of recipes? These books are the result of the cooperation of over 400 people in the wine industry. In 1961 the Wine Advisory Board began collecting the favorite and best recipes of various winemakers and their families. Most of the recipes are old family favorites, tested with time and then retested and proven in Wine Advisory Board test kitchens. We are particularly pleased with the recipes and wine choices from staff members of the Department of Viticulture and Enology and the Department of Food and Science and Technology of University of California, Davis and Fresno.

#501 Gourmet Wine Cooking The Easy Way: Recipes for memorable eating, prepared quickly and simply with wine. Most of the recipes specify convenience foods which can be delightfully flavored with wine enabling the busy lay chef to set a gourmet table for family & friends with a minimum of time in the kitchen. More than 500 tested and proven recipes; used frequently by the first families of America's wine industry. 128 pp, 8 1/2" x 11", illustrated 2001 edition $12.95 @ 2 ISBN 0-932664-01-6

#502 New Adventures in Wine Cookery by California Winemakers: 2001 Edition includes many new recipes from California's new winemakers. The life work of the winemakers is to guide nature in the development in wine of beauty, aroma, bouquet and subtle flavors. Wine is part of their daily diet, leading to more flavorful dishes, comfortable living, merriment and good fellowship. These recipes contributed by Winemakers, their families and colleagues represent this spirit of flavorful good living. A best selling cookbook with 500 exciting recipes including barbecue, wine drinks, salads and sauces. 128 pp, illustrated, 81/2" x 11", $12.95 @ ISBN 0-932664-10-5.

#503 Favorite Recipes of California Winemakers: The original winemaker's cookbook and a bestseller for fifteen years. Over 200 dedicated winemakers have shared with us their love of cooking. They are the authors of this book, which is dedicated to a simple truth known for thousands of years in countless countries: good food is even better with wine. Over 500 authentic recipes, many used for generations, are included in this "cookbook classic". 128 pp, 81/2" x 11", illustrated, $12.95 @ ISBN 0-932664-03-2.

#504 Dinner Menus with Wine by Emily Chase and Wine Advisory Board. Over 100 complete dinner menus with recommended complimentary wines. This book will make your dinner planning easy and the results impressive to your family and most sophisticated guests. Emily Chase worked with the winemakers of California a number of years and was also the Home Economics Editor of Sunset Magazine. She tested recipes for six years and is the author of numerous articles and books on cooking. This edition contains 400 different recipes, suggestions for wines to accompany dinners and tips on serving, storing and enjoying wine. 128 pp, illustrated, 8 1/2" x 11", $12.95 @ ISBN 0-932664-30-x.

#640 The Champagne Cookbook: "Add Some Sparkle to Your Cooking and Your Life" by Malcolm R. Hebert. Cooking with Champagne is a glamorous yet easy way to liven up your cuisine. The recipes range from soup, salads, hors d'oeuvres, fish, fowl, red meat, vegetables and of course desserts all using Champagne. Many new entertaining ideas with Champagne cocktails, drinks and Champagne lore are included along with simple rules on cooking with and serving Sparkling Wines. California, New York and European Champagne makers and their families provide recipes. The author's 30 years of teaching and writing about food and wine makes this an elegant yet practical book. 128 pp, illustrated, 81/2" x 11", $14.95 @ ISBN 0-932664-65-2

#641 The Pocket Encyclopedia of California Wine: "The most useful little book on California wine yet" A convenient and thorough reference book that fits in vest pocket. Provides answers to most questions about California wines, the wineries, grape varieties and wine terms. Includes maps and a tasting note section. Handy to carry with you to restaurants, wine tastings and wine shops to make intelligent selections. Covers Arizona, Mexico and Hawaii. 336 pp, 73/4" x 31/2" $14.95 @ ISBN 0-932664-40-7.

#672 Wine in Everyday Cooking by Patti Ballard. Patti is the popular wine consultant from Santa Cruz who has been impressing winery visitors and guests for years with her wine recipes and the cooking tips from her grandmother. Chapters range from soup and hors d'oeuvres through pasta and deserts—all of course with wine as an ingredient. 128pp, illustrated, $12.95 @ ISBN 0-932664-45-8.

#673 The California Wine Drink Book by William I. Kaufman. Cocktails, hot drinks, punches and coolers all made with wine. Over 200 different drink recipes, using various wines along with mixing tips and wine entertaining suggestions. Today's accent on lighter drinks makes this a most useful handbook and you'll save money too by using wine rather than higher taxed liquors. Pocket size, leatherette cover, 128 pp, and $6.95, ISBN 0-932664-10-9.

#727 Wine Lovers Cookbook by Malcolm Herbert, The most unique in our Wine Cookbook Series with 100 winning recipes from the National Cooking with Wine Contest. All recipes have been tested and written for easy preparation and reliable results. They range from the Artichoke Appetizer with Wine to cold Apricot Soup, Lime-house Chicken to Pumpkin Beef Stew. And in-depth chapter on California wine, a wine & food chart and cooking tips are included. With this book in hand the magic is out of the bottle. 176 pp, illustrated, 8 1/2" x 11". $12.95 @ ISBN 0-932664-82-2

#914 Wine, Food & the Good Life by Arlene Mueller & Dorothy Indelicato. "Celebrating 50 years of family winemaking." Here is a cookbook with generation proven, wine family recipes complemented by contemporary California cuisine recipes and wine entertaining tips. The California Wine Country lifestyle is captured through fascinating historical anecdotes from three generations of winemaking, old photos, and lots of sharing of cooking tips from the winemakers and their families. Recipes range from quick and easy to "gourmet' and represent a variety of ethnic background with Italian predominating. 144 pp, illustrated, 8 1/2"x 11". $12.95 @ISBN 0-932664-47-4

#6508 Pocket Encyclopedia of American Wine-Northwest by William I. Kaufman. The newest addition to Kaufman's award winning pocket encyclopedia series. Complete directory to all of the wineries in Oregon, Washington, Idaho, and Montana. Includes addresses, phone numbers, winemakers, owners and highlights on wines produced, varietals and vineyards. An essential and handy guide to the exciting new premium wine producing area. Leatherette cover, convenient 7 3/4' x 33 1/2', 160 pp. $7.95 @ISBN 0-932664-58-X

#6928 The Wine Buyer's Record Book, Ralph Steadman. The internationally popular cartoonist provides a handy and humorous little book to keep track of your wine tasting experiences, your cellar stock and other vinous notes. Steadman's whimsical art decorates the book in full color providing a chuckle as you make your notes. Sprial Bound, 5 x 7 1/2 inches, 64 pp. $9.95 ISBN 0-932664-98-9

#7372 The Science Of Healthy Drinking, Gene Ford, Foreword by Norman M. Kaplan, MD. The scientific evidence is mounting daily: Mode drinking is good for you! The vast majority of both men and women, young and old, will benefit from daily imbibing. Most important are the cardiovascular benefits of red wine. Moderate drinking reduces the occurrences of angina, atherosclerosis, blood clots, coronary artery disease, strokes and heart attacks. The surprising benefits of wine as an anti-oxidant, reducing Cancer morbidity and mortality are documented. Over 1500 studies and articles are cited as the science behind the 30 specific health benefits of moderate drinking: from Alzheimer's to Osteoporosis to Ulcers, from the Common Cold to Diabetes to Kidney Stones.Hardcover, 7X9 inches, 460pp, graphs, charts, extensive bibliography and inde. $29.95 ISBN 1-891267-47-7

HOW TO ORDER BY PHONE: 800 231-9463 or Fax 650 866-3513. Indicate the number of copies and titles you wish on the order form below and include your check, money order. or Master or Visa card number. California residents include 8.5% sale tax. There is a $5.00 S/H fee per order, regardless of how many books you order. (If no order form – any paper will do.) Mailing address 360 Swift Ave. South San Francisco, CA 94080.

Ship To: _____

Address: _____

*City*_____ *State*_____ *Zip*_____

Please send the following:

_____*Copies #501 Gourmet Wine Cooking The Easy Way $12.95 @*_____

_____*Copies #502 New Adventures In Wine Cookery $12.95 @*_____

_____*Copies #503 Favorite Recipes of California Winemakers $12.95 @*_____

_____*Copies #504 Dinner Menus With Wine $12.95 @*_____

_____*Copies #640 The Champagne Cookbook $14.95 @*_____

_____*Copies #641 Pocket Encyclopedia of California Wines $14.95 @*_____

_____*Copies #672 Wine In Everyday Cooking $12.95 @*_____

_____*Copies #673 California Wine Drink Book $6.95 @*_____

_____*Copies #727 Wine Lovers Cookbook $12.95 @*_____

_____*Copies #914 Wine, Food And The Good Life $12.95 @*_____

_____*Copies #986 Fine Wine In Food $12.95 @*_____

_____*Copies #6508 Pocket Encyclopedia of American Wines-Northwest $7.95 @*_____

_____*Copies #6928 The Wine Buyer's Record book $9.95 @*_____

_____*Copies #7372 The Science of Healthy Drinking $29.95 @*_____

California residents 8.5% sales tax _____

Plus $5.00 shipping and handling (per order) _____

Please charge to my Master card or Visa card # _____

*Expiration Date*_____

*Signature*_____